REVISE AQA GCSE
Spanish

REVISION GUIDE

Series Consultant: Harry Smith   Authors: Leanda Reeves and Tracy Traynor

THE REVISE AQA SERIES
Available in print or online

Online editions for all titles in the Revise AQA series are available Summer 2013.

Presented on our ActiveLearn platform, you can view the full book and customise it by adding notes, comments and weblinks.

Print editions

Spanish Revision Guide	9781447941187
Spanish Revision Workbook	9781447941224

Online editions

Spanish Revision Guide	9781447941194
Spanish Revision Workbook	9781447941231

Audio files
Audio files for the listening exercises in this book can be found at: www.pearsonschools.co.uk/mflrevisionaudio

This Revision Guide is designed to complement your classroom and home learning, and to help prepare you for the exam. It does not include all the content and skills needed for the complete course. It is designed to work in combination with Pearson's main AQA GCSE Spanish 2009 Series.

To find out more visit:
www.pearsonschools.co.uk/aqagcseMFLrevision

ALWAYS LEARNING   **PEARSON**

Contents

Audio files

Audio files and transcripts for the listening exercises in this book can be found at: www.pearsonschools.co.uk/mflrevisionaudio

A small bit of small print

AQA publishes Sample Assessment Material and the Specification on its website. This is the official content and this book should be used in conjunction with it. The questions in *Now try this* have been written to help you practise every topic in the book. Remember: the real exam questions may not look like this.

Target grades

Target grades are quoted in this book for some of the questions. Students targeting this grade should be aiming to get most of the marks available. Students targeting a higher grade should be aiming to get all of the marks available.

Birthdays

You need to recognise dates in reading and listening questions, so learn months and numbers!

Los cumpleaños

enero

febrero

marzo

abril

mayo

junio

julio

agosto

septiembre

octubre

noviembre

diciembre

Dates

Grammar page 107

Dates in Spanish are easy. You just use regular numbers. Don't forget to add the **de**.

- 5 de marzo de 2014   5 March 2014
- 21 de diciembre de   21 December
  2013   2013

The only exception is the first of the month:

el primero de abril   1 April

> You don't use a capital letter for months.

Mi cumpleaños es el trece de diciembre.
My birthday is on 13 December.

Nací / Nació el 8 de abril.
I / She was born on 8 April.

el día anterior   the day before
el día después   the day after

Worked example

 LISTENING 1   target B-C

LISTENING 21   Audio files
Audio files and transcripts can be found at:
www.pearsonschools.co.uk/mflrevisionaudio

Listen and answer the question.

When is Carlos's birthday?

A 12 July   B 6 July   C 13 July

A

Me llamo Carlos. Mi madre nació el trece de julio de mil novecientos ochenta y seis y, por casualidad, mi cumpleaños es el día anterior.

Listening for numbers

- Make sure you know the numbers 1 to 31 for dates.
- Listen carefully to distinguish between similar sounding numbers, e.g. once / doce (11 / 12), cinco / quince (5 / 15), seis / siete (6 / 7).
- Listen out for **mil** to help you identify dates, e.g. 2013 = **dos mil trece** and **mil** = 1000 e.g.

  1986 = **mil novecientos ochenta y seis**

Now try this

 LISTENING 2   target C

Listen to the whole recording and answer the questions.

1 In what year was Carlos's mother born?   A 1986   B 1968   C 1978 ☐

2 When is Francisco's birthday?   A 12 July   B 2 June   C 2 July ☐

3 When was Francisco's father born?   A 1963   B 1973   C 1983 ☐

Pets

Do you have any pets? This page helps you give your opinion on them.

Las mascotas

¿Tienes mascotas?   Do you have pets?

Tengo / No tengo ...   I have / don't have ...

un caballo   un canario   un gato   un pájaro

un periquito   un perro   un pez   una cobaya

un conejo   un ratón   una tortuga

Plurals

Grammar page 85

It's easy to make nouns plural in Spanish.

- Nouns ending in a vowel:

  un caballo ➡ dos caballos

  un pájaro ➡ cuatro pájaros

- Nouns ending in a consonant (except -z):

  un ratón ➡ cinco ratones

- Nouns ending in -z:

  pez ➡ peces

Nouns ending -ón or -ión have no accent in the plural.

If you're referring to who owns a pet, use the definite article (el / la / los / las) and de:

El perro de mi abuela es muy pequeño.

My grandmother's dog is very small.

Worked example

READING target C

Read the blogs on pets. Who has a dog?

Olivia

¡Hola! Me llamo **Tomás** y vivo en un pueblo en el norte de Mallorca. Me fascinan las mascotas y tengo dos gatos, tres conejos y ¡una tortuga muy antipática! Pronto nos vamos a comprar un perro porque nos encantan. A mi hermano odia los animales pero tiene tres peces.

¡Hola! Me llamo **Olivia** y vivo en México. En mi casa nos gustan mucho los animales domésticos. ¡Tenemos siete chihuahuas! Es verdad que tener siete perros es bastante trabajo pero los adoro. Mi hermana y yo tenemos que llevar a los perros de paseo dos veces al día.

Reading strategies

Remember to pick out the KEY VOCABULARY from the questions and then find and read the relevant sentence carefully.

Don't just concentrate on nouns as verbs are very important too!

- Here, Tomás mentions a dog but the verb he uses is **comprar** (to buy) rather than **tener** (to have): Pronto nos vamos a comprar un perro ... (Soon we are going to buy a dog ...).
- Olivia uses a different verb which is key to completing the task: **tener siete perros es bastante trabajo pero ...** (having seven dogs is a lot of work but ...)

Now try this

READING target C

Read the blog again and answer: **T** (Tomás), **O** (Olivia) or **T + O** (Tomás and Olivia). Who ...

1 has many animals at home? ☐

2 has a family member who does not like animals? ☐

3 has rabbits? ☐

4 helps look after the animals? ☐

Physical description

Describe yourself and your friends using this vocabulary. Remember to make adjectives agree!

La apariencia física

Tiene el pelo ...   He / She has ... hair

rubio y largo   castaño y largo

negro y corto

Es pelirrojo.	He has red hair.
Lleva gafas.	He / She wears glasses.
Lleva un pendiente.	He / She wears an earring.
Soy alto / bajo.	I'm tall / short.
Es gorda / delgada.	She is fat / slim.
Es guapo / feo.	He is good-looking / ugly.

Tengo los ojos azules / castaños / verdes.
I have blue / brown / green eyes.

Adjectival agreement
Grammar page 86

Adjectives describe nouns.
They must agree with the noun in gender (masculine or feminine) and number (singular or plural).

	Singular	Plural
Adjectives ending -o:		
Masculine	alt<u>o</u>	altos
Feminine	alta	altas
Adjectives ending in a consonant:		
Masculine	azu<u>l</u>	azules
Feminine	azul	azules

Remember: when you're describing hair and eyes, the adjectives need to agree with **pelo** and **ojos**, not with the person being described.

Worked example
LISTENING 3   target D

Alejandro is talking about his family.
Listen and write the correct letter in the box provided.
Alejandro's father has
A blond hair   **B** long hair   **C** curly hair.
☐ C

Listening strategies

Read the question FIRST so you know what to listen out for. You might not know the word rizado, but you can work out it's the answer by ruling out 'black' (negro) and 'long' (largo).

Me llamo Alejandro. Soy delgado y tengo el pelo negro. Mi padre tiene el pelo rizado.

Make sure you learn the Spanish words for family members so you know who is being described.

Now try this
LISTENING 4   target D

Listen to the rest of the recording and write the correct letters for Manu's family.

A	blue eyes
B	green eyes
C	blond hair
D	red hair

E	fat
F	slim
G	short

1 Mother ☐ ☐
2 Father ☐ ☐
3 Sister ☐

Character description

This page will help you describe people's personality. Remember to use ser for this.

La personalidad

activo	active
alegre	happy
simpático	friendly
generoso	generous
gracioso	funny
responsable	responsible
amable	kind
comprensivo	understanding
hablador	chatty
inteligente	intelligent

agresivo	aggressive
perezoso	lazy
sensible	sensitive
tonto	stupid
egoísta	selfish
nervioso	nervous
antipático	unfriendly
travieso	naughty
tímido	shy

Era gracioso.
He used to be funny.

Using ser (to be) to describe personality

Grammar page 93

	ser – to be (personality)
I am	soy
you are	eres
he / she / it is	es
we are	somos
you are	sois
they are	son

Soy amable.   I am kind.

Aiming higher

Use a wider range of vocabulary to achieve higher marks. Try to work in words like these:

atrevido	daring
celoso	jealous
maleducado	rude
orgulloso	proud
mentiroso	liar
glotón	greedy
cortés	polite

Worked example

SPEAKING

¿Cómo es tu amigo?
What is your friend like?

AIMING HIGHER

Mi mejor amigo se llama Roberto y a mi modo de ver es encantador. Antes era muy tímido, pero ahora es más hablador que yo, y a veces puede ser gracioso. Nunca es maleducado ni negativo y siempre nos ponemos de acuerdo. Tiene muchos amigos en el cole.

CONTROLLED ASSESSMENT

Examiners often say that one of the most common mistakes is confusion between **muy** (very), **más** (more) and **mucho** (much, a lot). Make sure you know when to use each correctly.

This student uses the **imperfect** and **present** tenses in the same sentence and also various **connectives**. These add interest and complexity to the opinion: **antes era muy tímido, pero ahora es más hablador que yo, y a veces puede ser gracioso** (he used to be very shy before but now he's more chatty than I am and sometimes he can be funny).

Now try this

SPEAKING

Talk about your friend. Aim to talk for at least a minute.

¿Cómo es tu amigo?

Brothers and sisters

This page will prepare you with lots of things to say about your brothers and sisters.

Mis hermanos

Mi hermano está casado.
My brother is married.

Me llevo bien con mi hermana.
I get on well with my sister.

Me llevo mal con mi hermanastro.
I don't get on well with my stepbrother.

Me parezco a mi hermana menor / mayor.
I look like my younger / older sister.

Tenemos una relación problemática.
We have a problematic relationship.

Nos gustan los mismos pasatiempos.
We like the same hobbies.

Tenemos una relación de amor y odio.
We have a love / hate relationship.

Tenemos el mismo sentido del humor.
We have the same sense of humour.

Le quiero mucho.   I love her / him a lot.

Discutimos mucho.   We argue a lot.

Reflexive verbs

Grammar page 92

Verbs which talk about relationships are very often reflexive verbs.

Se parece a mi madre.
He looks like my mother.

Me parezco a mi hermana.
I look like my sister.

Nos llevamos bien.
We get on well.

Using reflexive verbs will help you show a higher level of Spanish.

Worked example

SPEAKING

¿Te llevas bien con tu hermano?

Me llevo bien con mi hermano y le quiero mucho. Es muy gracioso y nos gustan los mismos pasatiempos, como el fútbol y la natación.

This version makes good use of a reflexive verb (**me llevo bien**) and an opinion (**es muy gracioso**).

AIMING HIGHER

Cuando éramos pequeños nos llevábamos mal y siempre discutíamos, pero ahora me llevo mejor con él ya que tenemos los mismos intereses y el mismo sentido de humor. A veces no nos ponemos de acuerdo pero tratamos de resolver cualquier problema de manera apropiada.

This version is more impressive as it introduces a second tense **nos llevábamos** (the imperfect), to describe what the relationship used to be like, and uses the **nosotros** form.

CONTROLLED ASSESSMENT

Not making any mistakes **doesn't** mean you'll automatically achieve a higher grade. To aim for a higher grade, you need to use more complex language and your pronunciation and intonation must be generally good.

Now try this

SPEAKING

Answer the question.

¿Te llevas bien con tu hermano/a?

Get a copy of the **mark scheme** for speaking. Look at marks for:
- communication (10)
- range and accuracy of language (10)
- pronunciation and intonation (5)
- interaction and fluency (5)

Extended family

This page will help you talk about your family. Make sure you can use possessive adjectives too.

La familia

padre   abuelo   madre   abuela

hijo   hija

madre (f)	mother
padre (m)	father
abuelo (m)	grandfather
abuela (f)	grandmother
hijo/a (m/f)	son / daughter
mi madrastra	my stepmother
mi padrastro	my stepfather
mi tío/a	my uncle / aunt
mis primos	my cousins
su marido / su esposo	her husband
su mujer / su esposa	his wife

Están prometidos / casados / separados / divorciados.
They're engaged / married / separated / divorced.

Possessive adjectives

> Grammar page 87

Possessive adjectives agree with the noun they describe, not the person who 'possesses'.

	m. sing.	f. sing.	m. pl.	f. pl.
my	mi	mi	mis	mis
your (sing.)	tu	tu	tus	tus
his / her / its	su	su	sus	sus
our	nuestro	nuestra	nuestros	nuestras
your (plural)	vuestro	vuestra	vuestros	vuestras
their	su	su	sus	sus

Examples:

mis padres	my parents
sus parientes	his / her / their relatives
nuestro/a primo/a	our cousin

Worked example

 READING   target C

How does this person describe their relationships with brothers and sisters? Write **P** (Positive), **N** (Negative) or **P + N** (Positive and Negative)

Tengo una hermanastra de quince años y no discutimos nunca. Nos queremos muchísimo.
Lucía

P

EXAM ALERT!

Pupils have struggled with this type of question as they have not understand small key words such as **siempre** (always), **nunca** (never), **de vez en cuando** (sometimes) and **sólo** (only).

Also remember that in this type of question, there will always be at least one P, one N and one P + N, and only one of the options will be repeated.

> Students have struggled with exam questions similar to this – **be prepared!**

Now try this

 READING   target C

Read the texts below and write **P** (positive), **N** (negative) or **P + N** (positive and negative).

1 Mi hermano mayor y yo pasamos momentos divertidos pero a veces no nos llevamos bien. Me critica mucho.
Adrián ☐

2 Me enfado con mi gemela porque me ofende mucho. Nos llevamos fatal. Estoy harto de ella.
Álvaro ☐

Friends

You can use this page to prepare your thoughts about friends and friendship.

Los amigos

Un buen amigo debe ...
A good friend should ...

saber escuchar — know how to listen

ayudar con problemas — help with problems

decir la verdad — tell you the truth

estar siempre a tu lado
always be by your side

recordar tu cumpleaños
remember your birthday

ser como un hermano
be like a brother

aceptarte como eres
accept you as you are

Creo que los amigos son importantes.
I think friends are important.

Es importante que los amigos se lleven bien.
It's important that friends get on well.

Los amigos están ahí para apoyarte.
Friends are there to support you.

La amistad es más importante que el amor.
Friendship is more important than love.

The verbs deber and saber

deber should	saber to know (information)
debo	sé
debes	sabes
debe	sabe
debemos	sabemos
debéis	sabéis
deben	saben

Un buen amigo debe ser honrado.
A good friend should be honest.

Un buen amigo sabe guardar tus secretos.
A good friend knows how to keep your secrets.

Worked example WRITING

Describe what makes a good friend

En mi opinión, un buen amigo debe estar siempre a tu lado y sabe guardar tus secretos. Debe aceptarte como eres. Creo que los amigos son importantes.

AIMING HIGHER Creo que un buen amigo siempre sabe escucharte y nunca te dirá mentiras. También debe estar siempre a tu lado y aceptarte como eres. Para mí los amigos son importantísimos porque nos dan confianza. Es importante que los amigos se lleven bien. A mi parecer, la amistad es más importante que el amor.

Introducing **opinions** (with **en mi opinión / creo que**) can help you achieve higher marks in the areas of communication and content.

- **Superlatives** (**es más importante que**) introduce more complex structures

- **Subjunctive clauses** (**se lleven bien** after **Es importante que ...**) show more complex language handled confidently.

Now try this WRITING

Describe your best friend.

Include **connectives** to make your work more coherent and fluent. Start your answer with something like **Mi mejor amigo es un buen amigo porque ...**

Daily routine

To talk or write about daily routines, make sure you review reflexive verbs and times.

Mi rutina diaria

Me levanto.	I get up.
Me ducho deprisa.	I shower quickly.
Me lavo la cara.	I wash my face.
Desayuno.	I have breakfast.
Salgo de casa.	I leave home.
Vuelvo a casa.	I get home.
Me relajo.	I relax.
Ceno.	I have dinner.
Me acuesto.	I go to bed.
Me duermo.	I go to sleep.

Me despierto a las siete.
I get up at seven o'clock.

Siempre estoy cansado.
I'm always tired.

Me visto y me pongo el uniforme.
I get dressed and put my uniform on.

Voy al instituto en coche.
I go to school by car.

Reflexive verbs

Grammar page 92

Remember: reflexive verbs have a PRONOUN before the verb: me levanto – I get up.

Talking about time

Son ...   It's ...
A ...   At ...

Note the exception:
Es la una.
It's one o'clock.
A la una.
At one o'clock.

las dos	las dos y cinco	las dos y cuarto

las dos y media	las tres menos cuarto	las tres menos diez

Worked example

WRITING

Describe your daily routine.

Me despierto a las siete y media todos los días, pero ayer me levanté a las ocho y llegué al colegio con una hora de retraso.

AIMING HIGHER

Normalmente me despierto temprano, a las seis, pero ayer me levanté a las siete porque estaba cansado. Mis padres se despiertan a las seis. Siempre me ducho pero mi hermana se baña. Se pasa demasiado tiempo en el cuarto de baño. ¡Ayer se pasó treinta minutos! Ojalá tuviera mi propio cuarto de baño.

Aiming higher

Using a RANGE OF TENSES accurately will improve your range of language.

To aim even higher:

✓ include extra information clearly and explain ideas and points of view

✓ introduce various structures and plan your writing carefully.

- This version has added his opinion of his sister's behaviour (**se pasa demasiado tiempo en el cuarto de baño**).
- It also deserves a higher grade as it includes a **complex structure** (**ojalá que tuviera ...**) to say he wishes he had his own bathroom.

Now try this

WRITING

Describe your daily routine. Aim to write at least 100 words.

Remember to bring in other family member's routines so you can show off your knowledge of **verb endings** in a variety of **tenses**.

Breakfast

This page will help you talk about breakfast and how important it is.

El desayuno

un desayuno saludable	a healthy breakfast
Nunca desayuno.	I never have breakfast.
Desayuno ...	I eat ... (for breakfast)
cereales	cereal
yogur	yoghurt
fruta	fruit
con mantequilla	with butter
huevos	eggs
salchichas	sausages
una tostada con mermelada	
toast with jam	
Bebo ...	I drink ...
leche	milk
un zumo	a fruit juice

un café

un zumo de naranja

un té

Days of the week

lunes	Monday
martes	Tuesday
miércoles	Wednesday
jueves	Thursday
viernes	Friday
sábado	Saturday
domingo	Sunday

To specify a particular day, use los:
Los sábados por la mañana desayuno tostadas y huevos.

por la tarde / noche	
in the afternoon / at night	
los fines de semana	at weekends
todos los días / a diario	every day
a menudo	often
de vez en cuando	sometimes

Worked example

 READING **target A-B**

Read and answer the question.

Un buen desayuno

¿Sabías que el desayuno es la comida más importante del día? Algunas personas no le dan importancia a esta comida porque no tiene hambre por las mañanas. Lo evitan todos los días. Los jóvenes que desayunan saludablemente (zumo, tostadas, leche o cereales) sacan buenas notas. El secreto de un buen desayuno es un desayuno saludable, equilibrado y sabroso. Además, no se debe consumir bebidas estimulantes como el café o el té porque nos afectan y pueden causar estrés.

What do some people do every day?
They skip breakfast.

Reading strategies

- Always read the TITLE carefully to get an idea of what the text is about.
- Use what you DO know to work out what you don't.
- Knowing higher-level vocabulary such as sacar buenas notas ('to get good grades') is key to understanding this question.

Recognising direct object pronouns is important in this text: **lo evitan** they avoid **it** (the breakfast).

Now try this

 READING **target A-B**

Read the text again and answer the questions.

1 What happens to young people who eat a healthy breakfast?
2 What is the secret of a good breakfast?
3 What is the recommendation on drinking tea or coffee?

Eating at home

Work in useful structures to make talking and writing about what you eat more interesting.

Comer en casa

la comida	lunch
la cena	evening meal
la merienda	snack / picnic

el pescado

las verduras / las legumbres

la fruta

el pollo

la carne

las patatas fritas

el arroz

la pasta / los espaguetis

la ensalada

dulce / sabroso	sweet / tasty
picante	spicy
asado / frito	roast / fried
tener hambre	to be hungry
tener sed	to be thirsty

To say how long you have been doing something

Grammar page 94

To say how long you have been doing something, you can use desde hace + present tense or llevo + the gerund.

Como alimentos ecológicos desde hace dos años.
I have been eating organic food for two years.

Llevo cinco meses comiendo pescado fresco.
I have been eating fresh fish for five months.

To say you have just done something

Use acabo de + infinitive.

Acabo de dejar de comer carne.
I have just stopped eating meat.

Worked example   LISTENING 5   target A

Listen to Paco. Write the correct letter in the box.

Paco...
A used to eat meat
B has never eaten meat
C still eats meat

A

Normalmente hago comidas sanas. Antes comía hamburguesas, patatas fritas y perritos calientes pero ya no me gusta el sabor. Además, soy vegetariano desde hace seis años.

Learning vocabulary

To prepare for your exam, you need to learn lots of vocabulary. Remember the technique:

- LOOK at the words and memorise them
- COVER the words
- WRITE the words
- LOOK again
- SEE how many you got right

Start by covering the English words. When you're confident, cover the Spanish words and see if you can remember them from the English prompts.

Now try this   LISTENING 6   target A

Listen to the whole recording. Write the correct letter in each box.

1 Paco does not like …   **A** food grown locally   **B** fast food   **C** seafood   ☐

2 Paco is planning to …   **A** Use local produce to cook with   **B** eat more fish   **C** buy a farm   ☐

Eating in a café

Make sure you revise plenty of café words – they may feature in the exam.

Comer en la cafetería

¿Qué va a tomar?	What would you like?
Voy a tomar...	I'll have...
agua con gas	sparkling mineral water
agua sin gas	still mineral water
un café (solo)	a black coffee
una limonada	a lemonade
un té	a tea
con azúcar / leche	with sugar / milk
un bocadillo	a sandwich
una hamburguesa	hamburger
un perrito caliente	a hot dog

un helado de vainilla / fresa / chocolate
a vanilla / strawberry / chocolate ice cream

Tapas

el chorizo	salami-type sausage
las gambas al ajillo	garlic prawns
los calamares	squid in batter
la paella	traditional Spanish rice dish
las patatas bravas	spicy potatoes
la tortilla española	Spanish omelete

High frequency words

Watch out for key, but easily overlooked, words that affect meaning.

té con limón	tea with lemon
té sin limón	tea without lemon
nunca	never
siempre	always
solamente	only
hasta	until
todo el mundo	everybody
salvo / excepto	except
a causa de	because of

En mi familia todo el mundo bebe té sin leche.

In my family everyone drinks tea without milk.

Siempre meriendo un bocadillo de jamón.

I always have ham sandwich as a snack.

Worked example

Listen and choose the correct summary for Ana.

A I find ice-cream cafés sociable.

B I find ice-creams unhealthy.

C I find ice-cream cafés expensive. ☐C☐

Me llamo Ana. No voy a la cafetería porque los helados nunca son baratos. Prefiero tomar un té con amigos en mi casa.

Listening strategies

- Read all the statements CAREFULLY and MORE than once. Think strategically. If the statement says 'expensive', you could be listening for 'not cheap' or 'cost a lot', etc.
- Think and make CONNECTIONS. The text may not feature the Spanish for the exact words in the question. e.g. Ana doesn't say caro, she says nunca son baratos (never cheap).

Now try this

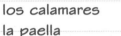

Listen to the rest of the recording. Say whether each person's opinion is **P** (positive), **N** (negative) or **P+N** (positive and negative).

1 Pablo ☐   **2** Miguel ☐   **3** María ☐

Eating in a restaurant

Use this vocabulary to talk about eating out in a restaurant.

Comer en el restaurante

el plato del día	set dish
el menú del día	menu of the day
la carta / el menú	menu
la cuenta	the bill
De primer plato...	For the first course...
De segundo plato...	For the second course...
De postre...	For dessert...
Para beber...	To drink...
una ensalada mixta	mixed salad
el gazpacho	cold tomato soup
una sopa de ajo	garlic soup
fruta del tiempo	seasonal fruit
pan y vino	bread and wine
¡Que aproveche!	Enjoy your meal!
Quiero quejarme.	I want to complain.
Está frío / poco hecho.	It's cold / undercooked.
Está demasiado salado.	It's too salty.

Using beber and comer in the preterite

Grammar page 95

	beber	comer
I / drank / ate	bebí	comí
he / she drank / ate	bebió	comió
we drank / ate	bebimos	comimos
they drank / ate	bebieron	comieron

Comimos en un restaurante para celebrar mi cumpleaños. Éramos dos. We ate in a restaurant to celebrate my birthday. There were two of us.

Worked example

READING · target B

Read this extract from Señor Vázquez's letter of complaint. Choose the correct summary.

Cenamos en su restaurante anoche y tuvimos muchos problemas. Habíamos reservado una mesa para las ocho y veinte pero estuvimos esperando media hora en el bar. Mi mujer pidió el bistec pero estaba poco hecho y el camarero nos trajo vino tinto en vez del vino blanco que pedimos. Quisimos un postre pero el camarero nunca llegó así que pedí la cuenta. Además, el camarero perdió mi abrigo y tuvimos que salir porque mi mujer estaba enferma.

Juan Vázquez

A The restaurant did not serve healthy food.
B The staff were not polite.
C The service was slow and the food undercooked. ☑ C

Understanding specific vocabulary is key to eliminating this summary. The wrong wine was brought (**nos trajo vino tinto en vez de vino blanco**) and the pudding was never ordered (**quisimos postre pero el camarero nunca llegó.**)

Now try this

READING · target B

Read the extract again. Which **three** of the statements are true? Write the correct letter in the boxes

A They went to their table twenty minutes late.
B They ate in the restaurant last night.
C The steak was undercooked.

D The waiter bought red wine instead of white.
E They all ate pudding
F They left without his wife's coat

☐ ☐ ☐

Healthy eating

Learn some key phrases from this page to give your opinion on healthy eating

La comida sana

Mi comida favorita es...
My favourite food is ...

la comida sana	healthy food
una dieta sana	a healthy diet
las sardinas	sardines
las nueces	nuts
la comida malsana	unhealthy food
los pasteles	cakes
los bombones / los caramelos	sweets
las galletas	biscuits
el chocolate	chocolate
Es sano.	It's healthy.
Es delicioso / rico.	It's delicious.
Es nutritivo.	It's nutritious.
Es malo para la salud.	It's unhealthy.
Contiene ...	It contains...
mucha grasa	a lot of fat
poca grasa	little fat

Using -ísimo for emphasis

Add -ísimo to the end of an adjective to make it stronger.

buenísimo	really good
riquísimo / sabrosísimo	extremely tasty

Work in your opinions using a wide range of expressions.

Creo que ... / En mi opinión ...
I think that ...

Me gusta ... / No me gusta ... / Odio ...
I like ... / I don't like ... / I hate ...

Creo que la comida española es buenísima.
I think Spanish food is really nice.

Worked example 🎧9 🎯B

Interview with a chef. Listen and write the correct letter in the boxes.

María thinks Spanish food is

A healthy   **B** greasy   **C** delicious.

☐ A

¡Hola! Me llamo María, soy cocinera y trabajo en un restaurante español en Londres. Cocino platos típicamente españoles. Lo bueno de la comida española es que es sana y contiene menos grasa que la comida china.

EXAM ALERT!

Multiple-choice questions are very common. Some pupils struggle when they hear words from each option mentioned. You need to listen carefully to the detail.

Students have struggled with exam questions similar to this – **be prepared!**

Understanding the adjective **sana** = healthy means you can answer question 1.

Now try this 🎧10 🎯B

Listen to the whole recording. Write the correct letter in the boxes.

1 María thinks Chinese food
   A isn't healthy
   B isn't greasy
   C isn't better than Spanish food.
   ☐

2 María eats
   A in her own restaurant
   B food cooked by her boyfriend
   C Spanish food.
   ☐

3 María thinks French food is
   A nutritious
   B greasy
   C tasty.
   ☐

Keeping fit and healthy

Use this page to prepare yourself to discuss healthy living.

Estar en forma

¿Qué haces para estar en forma?
What do you do to keep fit and healthy?

Es importante …	It's important …
hacer aerobic	to do aerobics
hacer ejercicio	to do exercise
dormir más	to sleep more
beber agua	to drink water
mantenerse en forma	to keep fit / healthy
comer fruta y verduras	eat fruit and vegetables
nunca fumar cigarrillos	never to smoke cigarettes
evitar la comida basura	to avoid junk food
nunca tomar drogas	never to take drugs
ser vegetariano	to be a vegetarian
no beber alcohol	not to drink alcohol
no estar estresado	not to be stressed
porque es peligroso	because it is dangerous
porque es asqueroso	because it is disgusting
malsano	unhealthy

Using Ojalá to say 'Let's hope!'

Ojalá is a word which means 'let's hope' or 'if only'. It is always followed by the subjunctive.

Ojalá no fumes más.
Let's hope you don't smoke any more.

Ojalá puedas dejar de comer tantos caramelos.

Let's hope you can stop eating so many sweets.

Ojalá pudiera estar más en forma.
If only I could be more fit and healthy.

These are all useful expressions to include if you want to aim for a higher grade.

Worked example

 SPEAKING

¿Qué haces para estar en forma?

Siempre duermo mucho y como verduras. Comía comida basura y bebía cerveza. En el futuro, comeré más verduras.

This student shows off their knowledge of **tenses**: **duermo, comía, comeré**, (present, imperfect and future) which will allow them to achieve higher in the range of language category.

AIMING HIGHER   Normalete duermo por lo menos ocho horas cada noche. También trato de comer verduras dos veces al día. Antes comía comida basura y bebía cerveza. En el futuro, comeré más verduras. Me gustaría relajarme más y es aconsejable dormir al menos ocho horas; así que seguiré este consejo. Ojalá pudiera estar más en forma.

Giving a **longer** response with more information (wanting to relax; sleeping at least eight hours) improves the communication mark. The use of more **complex** and **sophisticated language** (especially the **Ojalá** phrase about wanting to be fit) shows the ability to use a range of structures confidently.

Now try this

 SPEAKING

Answer the question. **¿Qué haces para estar en forma?**

You could mention:
* what you normally do to keep fit and healthy
* what you used to do
* what you will do
* if you have any bad habits.

Health problems

The language here will help you tackle listening or reading tasks on health problems.

Problemas de salud

ser adicto	to be an addict
estar borracho	to be drunk
un hábito	a habit
la terapia	therapy
respirar	to breathe
morir	to die
inyectar / una inyección	to inject / an injection
adelgazar	to lose weight
engordar	to gain weight
fumar (un porro)	to smoke (a spliff / joint)
tomar drogas	to take drugs
parar / dejar de fumar	to stop smoking
dificultades respiratorias	breathing dificulties
cáncer de pulmón	lung cancer
la droga blanda	soft drugs
la droga dura	hard drugs
resistir la tentación	to resist temptation
tener miedo	to be scared
tener dolor de	to have a pain in the ...

Using para to extend sentences

Grammar page 104

Using para + the infinitive will allow you to extend your sentences and aim for a higher mark.

Fumo para relajarme.   I smoke to relax.

He dejado de fumar para respirar mejor.
I have stopped smoking to improve my breathing.

For higher grades, try using these phrases in your controlled assessment:

Beben alcohol para olvidarse de sus problemas.
They drink alcohol to forget their problems.

Para resistir la tentación de fumar, no salgo con amigos que fuman.
Nunca lo probaría.
In order to resist the temptation to smoke, I don't go out with friends who smoke. I would never try it.

Worked example

 LISTENING 11   target A-A*

A radio programme. Listen and write the problem identified.

smoking

Una encuesta reciente revela que para los padres el tabaquismo sigue siendo una gran preocupación.

EXAM ALERT!

This type of question is one that students often struggle with. For example, here they may struggle with identifying the problem "smoking" from the word **tabaquismo**. To avoid this, learn your vocabulary carefully!

Students have struggled with exam questions similar to this – **be prepared!**

Now try this

 LISTENING 12   target A-A*

Which problems do these young Spanish people worry about? Listen and write the problems.

1 ....

2 ....

3 ....

Remember to always write your answers in English, if you are asked the question in English. Writing **drogas** would not get any credit.

Future relationships

Relationship vocabulary is quite tricky, so make sure you learn the key phrases.

Las relaciones futuras

el amor	love
el chico / la chica	boy / girl
el novio / la novia	boy / girlfriend
el adulto	adult
el bebé	baby
el beso	kiss
el casamiento / matrimonio	marriage
la pareja	couple
la igualdad	equality
la independencia	independence
enamorarse	to fall in love
casarse	to get married
separarse	to get separated
divorciarse	to get divorced
estar casado/a	to be married
estar soltero/a	to be single
estar divorciado/a	to be divorced
Te quiero.	I love you.

Ser and estar

Grammar page 93

You will know that ser is used with descriptions:

Somos novios.
We are going out with each other.

Mi mejor amiga es bastante valiente.
My best friend is quite brave.

However, when you describe your relationship you use estar:

Estoy soltero pero mi amigo está casado.
I am single but my friend is married.

Mis padres están divorciados.
My parents are divorced.

Worked example

Read the text. Complete the sentences. Write the correct letter in the box.

> Vivo en casa con mi madre porque mis padres se han divorciado. En el futuro, creo que será más interesante vivir sola para independizarme. No sé si me casaré. Depende.
> **Lucía**

Lucía plans to

A live alone. **B** get married. **C** live with her boyfriend.

A

Aiming higher

Try reading online newspaper and magazine articles to get yourself used to more complex texts.

Make sure you are familiar with the key verbs and tenses for every topic. Here **No sé si me casaré.** means 'I don't know if I will get married', therefore the correct answer is 'she wants to live alone' as she says it will be more interesting to live alone.

Now try this

Complete the sentences. Write the correct letter in the box.

> Yo quería tener bebés cuando nos casamos hace dos años pero decidimos comprar un gato. Ahora nos vamos a separar y creo que tenemos suerte de no haber tenido hijos porque no me gustaría ser madre soltera. **Ana**

1 Two years ago, Ana **A** bought a dog. **B** had a baby. **C** got married. ☐

2 Ana is going to **A** be a single mother. **B** get separated. **C** have a baby. ☐

Social issues

If you are aiming for a high grade, you should be able to say something about important social issues.

Las cuestiones sociales

preocuparse de	to be worried about
la identidad	identity
la violencia	violence
el vandalismo	vandalism
los jóvenes violentos	violent youths
el racismo	racism
la probreza	poverty
el paro	unemployment
estar en paro	to be unemployed
maltratar a ...	to treat ... badly
los inmigrantes	immigrants
los extranjeros	foreigners
la juventud	the youth
la gente pobre	poor people
emigrar	to emigrate
los voluntarios	volunteers
el trabajo voluntario	voluntary work
la ONG	charitable organisation (NGO)

The present subjunctive

Grammar page 101

Learn ways you can add the subjunctive to your speaking and writing.

Es importante que acabemos con el racismo.
It's important that we stop racism.

Es esencial que protejamos a los inmigrantes.
It's essential that we protect immigrants.

Es necesario que encontremos soluciones a la violencia entre los jóvenes
It's necessary that we find solutions to violence between young people.

Worked example

What is this person writing songs about? Choose the correct theme.

Generalmente escribo canciones sobre los parados. Mucha gente no puede independizarse porque no tiene empleo.

A Homelessness D Immigration
B War   E Drugs
C Unemployment F Street crime

C

Aiming higher

✓ Understanding complex vocabulary and knowing your tenses thoroughly are key to unlocking texts at this level.

✓ Grouping together synonyms and linking themes is extremely useful in helping us deduce meanings in texts. For example,

muerto (dead)   peleas (fights)
la violencia
(violence)
miedo (fear)   pelearse (to fight)

Now try this

Choose the correct theme (A–F above) for these people.

1 Espero que mi música muestre que estoy en contra de los que inquietan a los vecinos en las calles con vandalismo, peleas y armas. Si no hacemos nada, más gente les va a tener miedo. ☐

2 Para mí la música tiene que hablarnos de lo que nos preocupa. Para mí, las substancias químicas llegan a ser el problema principal para la juventud de hoy y hay que protestar en voz alta. ☐

Social problems

Don't be afraid of talking about complex issues. Learn key nouns and verbs so that you can give interesting opinions on them.

Los problemas sociales

los 'sin techo'	the homeless
el drogadicto	drug addict
el gamberro	hooligan
el síndrome de abstinencia	withdrawal symptoms
el ciberespacio	cyberspace
la prensa	the press
el terrorismo	terrorism
los derechos humanos	human rights
la solidaridad	solidarity
la obra benéfica	charity
ocuparse de	to concern yourself with
cansar de	to be tired of
inquietarse de	to worry about
quejarse de	to complain about
participar en	to take part in
dar (mi / tu) tiempo	to give (my / your) time
aumentar	to increase
a causa de / debido a	due to
de hecho	in fact
sin embargo	however

Relative pronouns
 Grammar page 87

Think of different ways you can link together exciting verbs and vocabulary to express some complex opinions and ideas:

que	which that who
donde	where
como	like / as
cuando	when
cuyo	whose

Mucha gente cansa de los gamberros cuyo comportamiento violento aumenta cada día.
Many people are tired of hooligans whose violent behaviour increases daily.

El ciberespacio es donde mucha gente se queja de la prensa.
Cyberspace is where many people complain about the press

Worked example

 LISTENING 13  target A

What is Paco's opinion? Listen and write P (positive), N (negative) or P+N (positive and negative).

P + N

Mucha gente se queja de la juventud de hoy, diciendo que son torpes y perezosos y a veces es verdad. Sin embargo, por lo general no estoy de acuerdo porque todos mis amigos son amables y responsables.

You won't find the words 'positive' or 'negative' in the text. You need to look **carefully** to see the types of opinion Paco expresses. **Small words** can affect the meaning of a sentence. Look out for:

pero	but
sin embargo	however
(no) estoy de acuerdo	I (don't) agree
por lo general	generally
a veces	sometimes

Now try this

 LISTENING 14 target A

Listen to the whole recording. Where do Paco's friends do voluntary work?
Write the correct letter in each box.

A Charity shop
B Children's playgroup
C Animal rescue centre

D Home for the elderly
E Homeless charity
F Environmental group

1 Sofía ☐   **2** Jorge ☐   **3** Laura ☐

Hobbies

Prepare to talk and write about hobbies using this page. Research any hobbies not covered here.

Los pasatiempos

Toco la guitarra.

Bailo.

Leo.

Cocino.

Dibujo.

Pinto.

Voy al cine.

Juego al ajedrez.

Juego con videojuegos.

Salgo con amigos.

Veo deporte en la televisión.

Voy de pesca.

Present tense (regular verbs)

 Grammar page 91

To form the present tense of regular verbs, replace the infinitive ending as follows:

	hablar – to speak	comer – to eat	vivir – to live
I	hablo	como	vivo
you	hablas	comes	vives
he / she	habla	come	vive
we	hablamos	comemos	vivimos
you	habláis	coméis	vivís
they	hablan	comen	viven

Escucha música.   She listens to music.

- Tocar, bailar, cocinar, dibujar and pintar are all regular -ar verbs and leer is a regular -er verb.
- Ver, juegar, salir and ir are all verbs with **irregularities** in the present tense.

Worked example

 LISTENING 15 target F

Listen. What does Raúl like doing?

A Reading
B Playing tennis
C Playing football
D Listening to music
E Going swimming
F Going shopping

☐ C

Raúl juega al fútbol los sábados

Before you listen, try to predict what you're going to hear. Write the Spanish next to the English so you know what to listen out for.

EXAM ALERT!

Some students struggle with basic vocabulary such as **va de compras** and **natación**. Knowing basic words and phrases is crucial to performing well in listening. Make sure you're familiar with verbs used with sports: **jugar / practicar / hacer**.

Students have struggled with exam questions similar to this – **be prepared!**

Now try this

 LISTENING 16   target F

What do these other people like doing?

Listen and write the correct letter in the box.

1 Laura ☐   2 Pablo ☐   3 José ☐

Sport

When you're talking about sport, remember to use the appropriate verb – jugar / practicar / hacer.

Los deportes

¿Qué deporte practicas?
What sport do you do?

Juego ...	I play ...
al fútbol	football
al baloncesto	basketball
al tenis	tennis

Practico ...	I do ...
el atletismo	athletics
el ciclismo	cycling
el esquí	skiing
el footing	running
la equitación	horseriding
la gimnasia	gymnastics
la natación	swimming

Hago ...	I do ...
vela	sailing
patinaje	skating
un campeonato	a championship

Using jugar and practicar in different tenses

You use different verbs with different sports.

	jugar	practicar	hacer
Present	juego	practico	hago
Preterite	jugué	practiqué	hice
Imperfect	jugaba	practicaba	hacía
Future	jugaré	practicaré	haré

Jugaba al squash pero ahora no hago deportes. El año que viene haré vela.

I used to play squash but now I don't do any sport. Next year I'll do sailing.

Use phrases similar to these to aim for a top grade:

He jugado al voleibol pero no me gustó.
I have played volleyball but I did not like it.

Si pudiera, participaría en los Juegos Olímpicos.
If I could, I'd take part in the Olympics.

Worked example

READING   target A

Read the text.

Me llamo Roque y vivo en Zaragoza. Antes practicaba la equitación con mi hermana pero no le gustó. Ahora siempre practico la equitación tres veces a la semana pero no me gusta nada la natación y por eso no la hago nunca. Pero a mi hemanastro le encanta la natación. Para mí, la equitación es emocionante porque es un deporte rápido. En enero participaré en un campeonato y será divertido. Me gustaría ganar. Si pudiera, participaría en los Juegos Olímpicos.

According to Roque, which of these statements is true? ☐ B

A He used to do swimming.
B His sister used to do horse-riding with him.

Exam tips

- Understanding OPINION phrases in different tenses is very important. Look out for expressions using gustarse, such as no le gustó (she didn't like it) and phrases like será divertido (it will be fun).

- Key TIME REFERENCES, such as antes (before) or ahora (now) will also help you understand the detail.

Now try this

READING   target A

Read the text again. Which **two** statements are true? Write the correct letters in the boxes.

C He likes horse riding because it's an emotional sport
D He will take part in a competition in the new year

E He's not interested in winning a competition
F Competing will be fun

☐ ☐

Arranging to go out

If your school has Spanish visitors, you may well need to use vocabulary on this page to invite them to go out!

Las invitaciones para salir

¿Estás libre?　　　　Are you free?

¿Quieres salir el sábado?
Do you want to go out on Saturday?

Podemos / Me gustaría ir...
We could / I'd like to go...

al cine / a la bolera / a la piscina
to the cinema / bowling alley / swimming pool

¿Dónde nos encontramos?
Where shall we meet?

¿Nos encontramos en el café?
Shall we meet in the café?

Podemos quedar en la estación.
We can meet at the station.

No puedo, estoy ocupado.
I'm sorry, I'm busy.

¿A qué hora?　　　　At what time?

No puedo salir.　　　I can't go out.

No me apetece.　　　I don't fancy it.

Tengo que ...　　　　I have to ...

hacer los deberes　　do my homework

salir con mis padres　go out with my parents

hacer de canguro　　babysit

Stem-changing verbs

Grammar page 91

In stem-changing verbs, the vowel in the first syllable changes in the singular and the 3rd person plural.

	poder – to be able	querer – to want
I	puedo	quiero
you	puedes	quieres
he / she / it	puede	quiere
we	podemos	queremos
you	podéis	queréis
they	pueden	quieren

Both verbs are followed by the infinitive:

¿Quieres ir al cine el viernes?
Do you want to go to the cinema on Friday?

Worked example

Listen and write the correct letter in each box.

Juan suggests going to the

A sports centre
B disco
C cinema

☐ C

¡Buenas tardes, Lola! ¿Quieres salir el domingo? No puedo hacer deporte ni bailar porque me he roto la pierna pero, si quieres, podemos ir al cine con mi primo.

EXAM ALERT!

Students often make silly mistakes by not understanding times in listening exams. Times come up in all sorts of contexts – make sure you are completely confident in understanding and using them.

Students have struggled with exam questions similar to this – **be prepared!**

Now try this

Listen to the whole recording and complete the activity.

1 Juan is bringing his
　A cousin　B mother　C father ☐

2 Lola would prefer to go on
　A Friday　B Sunday　C Tuesday ☐

3 She suggests meeting at
　A 7.50　B 8.00　C 8.10 ☐

Had a look ☐ Nearly there ☐ Nailed it! ☐

Last weekend

Use the phrases here to write or talk about what you did last weekend.

El fin de semana pasado

Jugué al golf.	I played golf.
Hice mis deberes.	I did my homework.
Navegué por internet.	I surfed the internet.
Fui a una fiesta.	I went to a party.
Leí una revista.	I read a magazine.
Me quedé en casa.	I stayed at home.
Vi la televisión.	I watched TV.
Escuché mi iPod.	I listened to my iPod
Salí con mis amigos.	I went out with friends.
ayer	yesterday
el sábado pasado	last Saturday
el domingo pasado	last Sunday
el día después	the day after

Preterite tense

Grammar page 95

To form the preterite tense of regular verbs, replace the infinitive ending as follows:

	hablar to speak	comer to eat	vivir to live
I	hablé	comí	viví
you	hablaste	comiste	viviste
he / she / it	habló	comió	vivió
we	hablamos	comimos	vivimos
you	hablasteis	comisteis	vivisteis
they	hablaron	comieron	vivieron

Compré ropa.
I bought clothes.

Habló con sus amigas.
She talked to her friends.

Worked example

WRITING

Write about what you did last weekend.

Me encanta practicar la natación durante mi tiempo libre. A veces juego al baloncesto con mis amigos. El fin de semana pasado no jugué al baloncesto porque jugué al hockey con mis primos. Este fin de semana jugaré al tenis por la tarde.

AIMING HIGHER

Normalmente nunca juego al golf los fines de semana porque es aburrido y prefiero jugar al baloncesto. Sin embargo, el fin de semana pasado no jugué al baloncesto sino jugué al hockey y fue muy divertido. Es más, el fin de semana que viene jugaré al tenis con Ana. Será un partido interesante.

Going beyond the question to include **three tenses** helps you improve your level for the content and language categories. Using **connectives** (**porque**) and negatives (**no jugué**) to say what you didn't do at the weekend will also help you aim for a higher grade.

- Adding **opinions** (**porque es aburrido**) creates subordinate clauses which can help you aim higher in the 'knowledge of language' area.
- Using **more complex structures** (e.g. with **sino**) will also help you if you're aiming for a higher grade.

Now try this

WRITING

Write about what you did last weekend. Aim to write at least 100 words.
- Give details of any activities you did.
- Talk about what you usually do at the weekend.
- Outline your plans for next weekend.

TV programmes

You need to be able to describe the type of programmes you watch, as well as naming them.

Los programas de televisión

los programas de deporte
sports programmes

las noticias	news
los documentales	documentaries
los concursos	game shows
las series de policías / las policíacas	police series
los dibujos animados	cartoons
las telenovelas	soaps
un programa de tele-realidad	reality TV programme
Gran hermano	Big Brother

Aiming higher

For the top grades, you need to give and understand REASONS for your likes and dislikes. Use comparatives to impress!

The comparative

Grammar page 88

The comparative is used to compare two things. It is formed as follows:

más	+ adjective + que = more ... than
menos	+ adjective + que = less ... than

The adjective agrees with the noun it describes:

Las telenovelas son menos aburridas que los concursos.
Soap operas are less boring than gameshows.

Los dibujos animados son más interesantes que los programas de tele-realidad.
Cartoons are more interesting than reality TV programmes.

Worked example

READING   target C

Read the text and complete the table.

> Los programas de tele-realidad son divertidos y para mí son más interesantes que las telenovelas. *Concha*

Preferred type of programme	Reason
Reality TV	Fun and more interesting than soaps

Reading strategies

- Remember that if a table has headings in English, you must write in your answers in ENGLISH. Spanish will not be marked.
- Remember: never leave a blank. If you're unsure, have a guess. You might be right!

Read the text first to identify the type of TV programme. Then look for key adjectives to help you write the reasons. Here Concha uses **divertidos** and **más interesantes que las telenovelas** to give her opinions.

Now try this

READING   target C

Read the texts and note for each person their preferred type of programme and the reason.

> Creo que los documentales son más aburridos que los dibujos animados, que son graciosos. *Pablo*

> En mi opinión las noticias son más repetitivas que los concursos. Pienso que estos programas son más emocionantes. *María*

Cinema

Describing the last film you saw is a good topic for a speaking or writing assessment.

El cine

una comedia	a comedy
una película romántica	a romantic film
una película de dibujos animados	an animated film / cartoon
una película de acción	an action film
una película de ciencia ficción	a science-fiction film
una película de aventuras	an adventure film
una película de suspense	a thriller
una película de terror	a horror film
misterioso	mysterious
emocionante	exciting
fascinante	fascinating
raro	strange
sorprendente	surprising
impresionante	impressive
gracioso / cómico	funny
con subtítulos	with subtitles

The superlative

Grammar page 88

The superlative is used to compare more than two things. It is formed as follows:

El / la / los / las más + adjective = the most ...

El / la / los / las menos + adjective = the least ...

The definite article and the adjective agree with the noun described.

Las películas de terror son las más escalofriantes.
Horror films are the creepiest.

Note these irregular forms:
el / la mejor – the best
el / la peor – the worst
¡Las películas de aventuras son las mejores!
Adventure films are the best!

Worked example

Read Alejandro's opinion and write the correct letter in the box: **P** (positive), **N** (negative) or **P + N** (positive and negative).

En mi opinión, las películas de dibujos animados son las mejores porque son las más emocionantes. Además, algunas me hacen reír . **Alejandro**

☐ P

- Knowing the **superlative** (las más) is vital to understanding that Alejandro prefers cartoons
- Look for the adjectives to see the reason why. Look out for **porque** as a clue. He says they are **emocionantes** (exciting).

Now try this

Read these students' opinions about their hobbies. Write the correct letter in the box: **P** (positive), **N** (negative) or **P + N** (positive and negative).

Me gusta mucho ir al cine, pero depende de la película. Creo que las películas de aventuras son las mejores y lo bueno es que a veces son graciosas. Las películas del oeste son las peores porque son aburridas. **Sonia**

Los videojuegos me parecen tontos porque no son como la realidad y odio jugar con el ordenador todo el tiempo porque en mi opinión es muy aburrido. **Alberto**

Me encantan las películas. Las veo en casa con mi ordenador. Prefiero las películas de acción porque son muy cómicas. **Miguel**

Sonia ☐   Alberto ☐   Miguel ☐

Music

Make sure any discussion of music includes your opinions and some personal recollections.

La música

Estoy aprendiendo a tocar...
I am learning to play ...

Toco ...	I play ...
en la orquesta	in the orchestra
un instrumento	an instrument
el piano	the piano
en un grupo rock	in a rock group
la guitarra	the guitar
la música clásica	classical music

Grabo ...	I record ...
la música rock	rock music
la música folclórica	folk music
la música tradicional	traditional music
como el flamenco	like flamenco

Escucho canciones con mis amigos.
I listen to songs with my friends.

Mi cantante favorito se llama ...
My favourite singer is called ...

Using different verbs meaning 'to play'

Jugar and tocar both mean 'to play'. You use jugar for sports and tocar for musical instruments.

Juego al hockey.
I play hockey.

Juega al fútbol.
He / She plays football.

Toco el piano.
I play the piano.

Toca la batería.
He / She plays the drums.

Toca la guitarra.

Worked example 🎧 LISTENING 19 target A–A*

Pablo talks about his free time.
Where does Pablo go with his sister and what do they do there? (3 marks)

They go to the school music club. His sister sings and he plays the guitar.

At higher level, listenings will include addtional information, so read the question carefully. In this case, the key word is sister (**hermana**). Don't be distracted by what his **mejor amigo** (best friend) does.

(Pablo) Los jueves mi mejor amigo va al club de ajedrez pero yo no. Yo toco la guitarra en el club de música del instituto con mi hermana, que canta, mientras nuestro profesor toca el piano. Para mí, tocar un instrumento es lo mejor.

EXAM ALERT!

Some students lose out because they don't focus on verb endings carefully enough. Here it's very important that you distinguish between **toca** (he / she plays) and **toco** (I play). Not hearing negatives **pero yo no** (but not me) can also mean you get the wrong answer.

Students have struggled with exam questions similar to this – **be prepared!** ✏️

Now try this 🎧 LISTENING 20 target A–A*

Listen to Silvia and answer the questions.

1 Why is Silvia learning an instrument? Mention **two** things.

2 What is her favourite hobby?

New technology

Remember to include a wide range of online activities when you talk or write about this topic.

La tecnología moderna

Suelo ...	I usually ...
descargar música	download music
comprar por internet	buy online
hacer mis deberes	do my homework
chatear con mis amigos	talk to my friends
utilizar las salas de chat	use chat rooms
navegar por internet	surf the net
mandar fotos	send photos

ver videos en YouTube
watch videos on YouTube

subir fotos a Facebook
upload photos to Facebook

mandar correos electrónicos / mensajes (de texto)
send emails / texts

conectarse a la banda ancha
connect to broadband

el correo basura   spam

Talking about what usually happens

You use the verb soler + the infinitive to talk about what someone usually does.

suelo	I usually ...
sueles	you usually (singular / informal) ...
suele	He / she usually ...
solemos	we usually ...
soléis	you usually (plural / informal) ...
suelen	they usually ...

Suelo descargar música.
I usually download music.

Worked example

Listen and answer the questions
What activities does Miguel do online at the moment?

homework, send photos

Suelo hacer los deberes cuando estoy conectado a internet. Antes solía chatear con amigos pero ahora me parece aburrido. También suelo mandar fotos porque es más rápido.

- Recognising **suelo** in the present allows you to understand that doing homework and sending photos are in the **present**.
- Knowing that **solía** is a verb in the **imperfect** means that chatting with friends is an activity in the **past**.
- Take care not to jump to conclusions. In this context **ahora** means 'now' but refers to his opinion about the activity.

Now try this

Listen to the whole recording and answer the questions.

1 What did Miguel used to do online?
2 What online activities does Isabel do at the moment? Mention **two** things.
3 Why did she give up online shopping?

Internet language

Use this page to master internet language and review commands.

El lenguaje de internet

un chat	a chat room
una página web	a web page
el ciberespacio	cyber space
una contraseña	a password
descargar	to download
subir	to upload
adjuntar	to attach
guardar	to save
hacer clic	to click
mandar	to send
recibir	to receive
un correo electrónico	an email

Giving instructions

Grammar page 100

The imperative is used to give commands and instructions. It has a different form depending on whether the command is POSITIVE or NEGATIVE.

mandar to send	responder to answer	subir to upload
Positive: tú form minus s		
¡Manda! Send!	¡Responde! Answer!	¡Sube! Upload!
Negative: present subjunctive		
¡No mandes! Don't send!	¡No respondas! Don't answer!	¡No subas! Don't upload!

la pantalla

el teclado

el ordenador

el ratón

Worked example   target B

Read the advert and answer the question.

> ### Nuestros ordenadores son cada vez más útiles.
>
> - Sube fotos de tu fiesta
> - Descarga tu canción favorita (¡No descargues música ilegalmente!)
> - Manda un correo electrónico a tu tía en los Estados Unidos.
> ¡Haz clic aquí!
> Nunca olvides…
> - Trata con cuidado la pantalla y el teclado.
> - Guarda siempre tus documentos.
> - Lo mejor es que nadie conozca tu contraseña. No se la digas a nadie.

What does the advert suggest you upload?
your party photos

Reading strategies

- When answering questions in English you DON'T need to answer in full sentences. Often, three or four words will be enough.

- Look at the questions carefully and give EXACTLY the information asked for. Remember to give TWO pieces of information if the question is worth two marks, or if the example suggests that more than one word is needed.

Now try this   target B

Read the text again and answer these questions.

1 What advice does it give about downloading music?
2 What can you do using the email function?

3 What does it advise you to treat with care?
4 What does it tell you not to do with your password?

Internet pros and cons

Use these phrases to prepare your thoughts on the pros and cons of the internet.

Internet: las ventajas y los inconvenientes

mandar y recibir mensajes
to send and to receive messages

conversar con la familia en el extranjero
to talk with family abroad

comprar y vender por internet
to buy and to sell online

jugar a videojuegos con amigos
to play videogames with friends

el peligro de   the danger of

conocer a gente con malas intenciones
to meet people with bad intentions

el acoso escolar en las redes sociales
bullying on social networking sites

acceso a tus datos personales
access to personal data

Using ser in different tenses

Recognising ser (to be) in the past, present and future is key for higher-level reading questions.

Present	Imperfect	Future
soy	era	seré
eres	eras	serás
es	era	será

Escuchar y ver música por internet es guay.
Listening to and watching music online is cool.

Worked example

Read the article.

> Es obvio que existe mucho por resolver con respecto a Internet. Hace cinco años el problema más grave era el acoso escolar en las redes sociales pero los expertos dicen que actualmente el problema más serio es el peligro con las cuentas bancarias por internet. También dicen que dentro de diez años el contenido peligroso será el problema más grave. Quién sabe lo que pasará en el ciberespacio después de veinte años, pero es cierto que habrá problemas que afrontar.

Read and choose **one** correct statement. ☐ A

A There are lots of problems with the internet.
B Online bullying is the most serious problem at the moment.

- Knowing ser in the present, imperfect and future will enable you to distinguish between the problems.
- Time phrases antes (before), actualmente (currently) and dentro de diez años (in ten years) can also help distinguish time frames.

Now try this

Read the text again and choose **three** correct statements. ☐ ☐ ☐

A Social networking sites are places where cyberbullying occur.
B Online bank accounts are now a bigger problem than online bullying.
C In twenty years, there will be no online risks
D Shopping online will always be the main problem.
E In ten years time dangerous content will be the biggest risk.
F The biggest problem we face in the next ten years is the future of online banking.

Shops

Make sure you learn the names of shops. This will help you give and understand directions.

Las tiendas

un estanco	a tobacconist
un supermercado	a supermarket
una carnicería	a butcher's
una droguería	a shop selling household goods
una joyería	a jeweller's
una papelería	a stationer's
una peluquería	a hairdresser's
una tienda de muebles	a furniture shop
una tienda de comestibles	a grocer's
unos grandes almacenes	department stores

Cognates

- Look out for cognates in Spanish. These are words that RESEMBLE or are the SAME AS words in English, e.g. farmacia – pharmacy, quiosco – (newspaper) kiosk.
- Look out for ways to CONNECT Spanish words, too. This will help you work out the meaning of new words and help you remember vocabulary, e.g.

pescado – fish – pescadería – fishmonger's

juguete – toy – juguetería – toyshop

pan – bread – panadería – bakery

una pastelería

una tienda de ropa

una librería = bookshop, not library

Worked example

READING **target E**

Read this sign in a department store and answer the question.

El Corte Español
Salamanca

Directorio
6 Cafetería. Restaurante. Terraza.
5 Peluquería. Muebles y Decoración.
4 Joyería. Discos. Estanco.
3 Moda Hombre y Mujer
2 Juguetes y Videojuegos
1 Floristería. Librería.

What floor would you visit to buy video games? 2

Reading strategies

- Look for cognates – use what you know in English AND Spanish (e.g. you might not know juguetes, but you do know jugar …)
- Use your head! Think about what's likely to appear on a shop sign – that means you can rule out a lot of options

- Read through the text looking for **cognates**, e.g. videojuegos – video games. That will help you work out the easier answers first.
- As you find each answer, **cross out** the department in the text. It will help you to have fewer options to work with.
- **Check** your answers when you've finished, to make sure you're happy with your choices.

Now try this

READING **target E**

Read the sign again, what floor would you visit to …

1 have a haircut? ☐
2 buy a man's jumper? ☐
3 buy a watch? ☐

4 buy a dictionary? ☐
5 buy a doll? ☐

Shopping for food

You will need to know words for quantities when you're shopping for food in Spain.

Comprar comida

¿Qué desea?	What would you like?
Deme ..., por favor.	Give me ..., please.
¿Algo más?	Anything else?
Nada más.	Nothing else.

el jamón
serrano

el jamón de
York

el pan

el pescado

las gambas

el queso

el salchichón

la leche

la mermelada

las galletas

las sardinas

los huevos

Quantities

In Spanish you use de (of) with quantities, even with grams and kilograms:

una lata de tomates	a tin of tomatoes
una barra de pan	a loaf of bread
una caja de galletas	a box of biscuits
una botella de agua	a bottle of water
un cartón de leche	a carton of milk
un paquete de caramelos	a bag of sweets
un bote de mermelada	a jar of jam
doscientos cincuenta gramos de ... 250 grams of ...	
quinientos gramos de ... 500 grams of ...	
medio kilo de ...	half a kilo of...
un kilo de ...	I kilo of ...
una docena de huevos a dozen eggs	

Worked example   LISTENING 23   target D

Listen and write the correct letter in each box.

1 The competition was on
A Saturday   B Sunday   C Monday

[B]

2 The competition was organised by
A the church   B the town hall
C the tourist office.

[B]

El domingo en la plaza de la Iglesia tuvo lugar la fiesta de la tortilla organizada por el ayuntamiento.

You might not know what el ayuntamiento means but you can use what you do know to work out the answer. Before you listen, think about the options and what the words would be in Spanish: you probably know 'church' – iglesia – and 'tourist office' – oficina de turismo – so you can rule those out. That leaves 'the town hall' – the correct answer!

Now try this   LISTENING 24   target D

Listen to the whole recording and complete the activity.

1 The winner received ☐
A fifteen euros.
B fifty euros.
C five hundred euros.

2 The extra ingredient in Paco's tortilla was ☐
A mushrooms.
B ham.
C cheese.

At the market

Make sure you know a wide range of words for food. It will help you make your answers more varied and interesting.

Comprar comida

un melocotón	a peach
un plátano	a banana
unas fresas	strawberries
una manzana	an apple
una naranja	an orange
una piña	a pineapple
unas uvas	grapes
una cebolla	an onion
unos champiñones	mushrooms
una col	a cabbage
una coliflor	a cauliflower
unos guisantes	peas
unas judías	beans
unas judías verdes	green beans
una lechuga	a lettuce
unas patatas	potatoes
unas zanahorias	carrots

The indefinite article

The indefinite article changes to match the gender and number of the noun.

masculine: un tomate (a tomato)

feminine: una pera (a pear)

The plural form of the indefinite article means 'some' or 'any'.

(masculine)   (feminine)
unos plátanos   unas cebollas

Worked example

READING   target **G**

What is on the shopping list? Write the **two** correct letters in the boxes. ☒A☒ ☒D☒

Unos tomates	Unas judías
Unas cebollas	Unas uvas
Unas zanahorias	Unos guisantes

A   B   C   D

EXAM ALERT!

Remember to choose two letters and never leave a blank. If you are not sure of an answer, make an intelligent guess!

Students have struggled with exam questions similar to this – **be prepared!**

Now try this

READING   target **G**

Look at this shopping list and the pictures in the Worked example. Write the **two** correct letters in the boxes. ☐ ☐

Unos plátanos	Unas manzanas
Unas naranjas	Unas zanahorias
Unos champiñones	Unas peras

Clothes and colours

You can talk about clothes in different contexts, so be ready to use a variety of tenses.

La ropa y los colores

un cinturón	a belt
un sombrero	a hat
un vestido azul	a blue dress
una camisa blanca	a white shirt
una camiseta	a T-shirt
una chaqueta	a jacket
unas botas	boots
el chándal	tracksuit
el pantalón corto	shorts
el bañador	swimming costume
unos zapatos	shoes
de algodón / de seda	cotton / silk

una falda

unas zapatillas de deporte

el pantalón

el vestido

unos vaqueros

unas sandalias

Using a variety of tenses

You can:

- say what you NORMALLY wear (present).
  Llevo una blusa.   I wear a blouse.

- say what you wore ON ONE OCCASION (preterite).
  Llevé unos guantes.   I wore some gloves.

- say what you USED TO wear (imperfect).
  Llevaba una corbata.   I used to wear a tie.

- say what you WILL wear (future).
  Llevaré una rebeca.   I will wear a cardigan.

Colours

●	verde	●	negro
●	amarillo	●	rosa
●	rojo	●	marrón
○	blanco	●	azul

Make sure the colour words agree and are placed **after** the item of clothing, e.g.
una falda negra
a black skirt

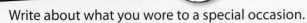

Worked example

WRITING

Write about what you wore to a special occasion.

Normalmente llevo vaqueros y camisetas pero para la boda de mi hermana llevé un vestido azul. Este fin de semana llevaré mi vestido nuevo para la fiesta de mi amigo.

AIMING HIGHER

Prefiero llevar ropa cómoda, como un chándal, porque es fácil, pero para la boda de mi prima llevé un traje azul de seda que era muy bonito. Me sentí segura de mí misma. Este fin de semana llevaré mi traje nuevo para la fiesta de mi amigo y estaré guapa.

Aiming higher

✓ You can use verbs in a variety of tenses:
Normalmente llevo …
Para la boda llevé …
Este fin de semana llevaré …

✓ Expressing an opinion in a past tense is good too. Why not try using the imperfect? e.g. Me encantaba llevar … I used to love wearing …

Now try this

WRITING

Write about what you wore to a special occasion. Write at least sixty words.

- Improve your answer by including an opinion using a **past tense**.
- Check that all your adjectives agree.

Shopping for clothes

If you're talking about clothes shopping, be ready to ask as well as to answer questions.

Comprar ropa

¿Me las puedo probar?	Can I try them on?
¿Qué tal le queda(n)?	How do(es) it / they fit?
No los / las tengo.	We don't have them.
Me los / las llevo.	I'll take them.
esta chaqueta	this jacket
estos vaqueros	these jeans

Me gustaría comprar estas botas negras.
I would like to buy those black boots.

¿Quiere probárselo?
Would you like to try it on?

¿Qué número / talla usa usted?
What size are you?

No lo / la tenemos en este tamaño.
We don't have them in this size.

Mi número de zapatos es el 39.
My shoe size is 39.

Busco un vestido, talla 38.
I am looking for a dress in size 38.

Estos zapatos son demasiado pequeños.
These shoes are too small.

> Remember: for size, use **talla** for clothes and **número** for shoes.

Quedar

Use the verb quedar to talk about how clothes fit you or suit you: queda for a SINGLE item and quedan for MORE THAN ONE.

La falda me queda bien.	The skirt suits me.
Las botas me quedan mal.	The boots don't suit me.

Direct object pronouns

	Masculine	Feminine
it	lo	la
them	los	las

– Estos zapatos son demasiado pequeños.
  Lo siento, no los tengo en su número.

Worked example

LISTENING 25 target C

Listen and complete the columns for number 1 in the table.

	Item	Problem	Colour purchased
1	skirt	too small	red
2			
3			

Hola. Me gustaría probarme esta falda roja pero esta talla me queda pequeña.

Listening strategies

- Remember to think about the vocabulary BEFORE you listen and anticipate key words to listen out for.
- KEY words to listen out for here are clothes, sizes and possible problems and colours.
- Don't forget to listen carefully for PRONOUNS!

If you can't remember straight away what **falda** means, write it down (in Spanish) next to the table and come back to it at the end. Sometimes you just need a little more time to help your brain find that word!

Now try this

LISTENING 26 target C

Listen to the rest of the recording and complete the table for numbers 2 and 3.

Returning items

Use this vocabulary to help you return problem items and refer to them accurately using demonstrative adjectives.

Devolver artículos

Quiero cambiar este / esta ...
I want to change this ...

Me gustaría devolver ...
I would like to return ...

Quiero hablar con el director.
I want to speak to the manager.

Quiero quejarme.	I want to complain.
Está estropeado.	It's broken.
Es demasiado grande.	It's too big.
Son demasiado pequeños.	They're too small.
Está roto.	It's broken.
Le falta un botón.	There is a button missing.
No le gusta a mi madre.	My mother doesn't like it.
No funciona.	It doesn't work.
Tengo el recibo.	I have the receipt.
Quiero un reembolso.	I want a refund.
Me parece inaceptable.	That's unacceptable.

Demonstrative adjectives

Grammar page 89

Demonstrative adjectives (this, that, these, those) are used with a noun and must agree with that noun.

	masculine	feminine
this / these		
singular	este	esta
plural	estos	estas
that / those		
singular	ese	esa
plural	esos	esas

este reloj   this watch
esta camiseta   this T-shirt

estas botas
these boots

estos zapatos
those shoes

Grammar page 89

Worked example

 LISTENING 27   target A

Listen and answer the question.
What problem does the man have with his recent purchase?

He bought shoes and a suit but the suit does not fit.

Compré estos zapatos y este traje la semana pasada en su tienda. Los zapatos me quedan muy bien pero el traje no.

EXAM ALERT!

If the questions are in English, you must answer in English! Check how many marks are awarded for each question and make sure you give enough information.

Students have struggled with exam questions similar to this – **be prepared!**

You may not understand every word in the dialogue. You need to focus on understanding the key phrases to answer the questions.

Now try this

 LISTENING 28   target A

Listen to the whole recording and complete the activity.

1 What is wrong with the item?
2 What does the man want the shop to do and why?
3 Why does the man have to come back tomorrow?

Shopping opinions

Not everyone likes shopping. Use the language here to help you give your opinion.

Opiniones sobre ir de compras

¿Te gusta ir de compras?
Do you like shopping?

Las ventajas de hacer compras por internet
the advantages of shopping online

Odio ir de compras.	I hate shopping.
Las desventajas ...	the disadvantages
las rebajas	sale
el precio	the price
ir / estar a la moda	to be fashionable
ir de compras	to shop
comprar / vender	to buy / to sell
hacer cola	to queue
bajo / caro / barato	low / expensive / cheap
gastar dinero	to spend money
el descuento	the discount

Try to work in different tenses:

Fui de compras.	I went shopping.
Compré ...	I bought ...
Compraré ...	I will buy ...
Volveré ...	I will return ...
Habrá ...	There will be ...

Negatives

Grammar page 102

no goes before the verb:

No voy.	I don't go.

Other negatives go either side of the verb, forming a sandwich:

nada	nothing, not at all
No tengo nada.	I have nothing (at all).
nadie	nobody
No hay nadie aquí.	There's nobody here.
nunca / jamás	never
No voy nunca a Londres.	I never go to London.
ni... ni...	neither... nor...
No me gusta ni el azul ni el verde.	I don't like blue or green.

No me gusta nada ir de compras.
I don't like shopping at all.

Worked example

¿Te gusta ir de compras?

Me encanta ir de compras para ver lo que hay en las tiendas de marca. Son impresionantes. Ayer fui a Manchester porque en mi pueblo no hay ninguna tienda de moda. Fue divertido.

AIMING HIGHER Siempre me fascina ir de compras, sobre todo para ver si las tiendas de marca tienen rebajas. Tienen ropa impresionante. Ayer fuimos a Londres porque en nuestro pueblo no hay ninguna tienda de moda. Fue genial porque gasté mucho dinero. Volveré la semana que viene porque vi un vestido precioso que creo que compraré.

Give your opinion about a past shopping trip to improve your content. The use of a preterite tense verb (**fui**) and a negative phrase (**ninguna tienda**) to describe the trip adds variety.

Here, the use of the future tense (**volveré, compraré**) to say that she will return to London and buy a new dress adds another tense and helps and helps aim even higher.

Now try this

¿**Te gusta ir de compras?** Answer in Spanish. Speak for about one minute.

You could mention:
- a recent trip and what you bought
- what you will buy in the future.

Pocket money

Pocket money is a topic which needs good knowledge of numbers. Make sure you know them.

La paga

Compro ...   I buy ...

 revistas

 caramelos

 ropa

 maquillaje

 pendientes

 libros / novelas

saldo para el móvil   credit for my mobile

Ahorro dinero.   I save money.

Recibo dos euros al día.   I get two euros a day.

a la semana   a week

al mes   a month

cada quince días   every fortnight

No malgasto el dinero.   I don't waste my money.

Es importante divertirse.

It's important to have fun.

Direct object pronouns

Grammar page 90

Use direct object pronouns to avoid repeating a noun.

¿Te gustan los caramelos? Sí, los compro cada quince días.

Do you like sweets?

Yes, I buy them every fortnight.

Recibo dinero de mis padres.

Lo ahorro para descargar música.

I get money from my parents. I save it to download music.

The pronoun agrees in number and gender with the noun it replaces:

	Singular	Plural
Masculine	el dinero ➡ lo	los pendientes ➡ los
Feminine	la ropa ➡ la	las novelas ➡ las

Worked example

 LISTENING 29   target B

Listen and answer the question.

What does she not spend her pocket money on?

Make up or concert tickets

... mis hermanas se lo gastan en maquillaje o entradas para conciertos pero yo no ...

Remember to listen out carefully for negatives. It's when she talks about her sisters that she tells us what she does **not** buy.

EXAM ALERT!

Where listening questions are numbered 1, 2, 3, etc., this means there will be a longer piece of recorded text without pauses after each one. However, If the text uses a), b), c), there will be a pause. Students have sometimes struggled because they have not realised they are expected to listen for all the answers in one go, and so have missed out on answering all the questions successfully.

Students have struggled with exam questions similar to this – **be prepared!**

Now try this

 LISTENING 30   target B

Listen to the whole recording and complete the activity.

1 Why does she save her money?
2 What did she used to do with her money?
3 Why won't she get pocket money from her parents next year?

In Question I the key verb forms to listen for are future or conditional, as she talks about future plans.

Holiday destinations

Use this page to talk about holidays and compare different places.

Dónde ir de vacaciones

Me gusta ir ...	I like to go ...
a la montaña	to the mountain
a la playa	to the beach
a nuestro piso en España	to our apartment in Spain
a estar con nuestra familia	to stay with our family
al extranjero	abroad
a sitios culturales	to cultural places

donde puedo practicar mi español
where I can practise my Spanish

Es más relajante / tranquilo.
It's more relaxing / peaceful.

Es menos concurrido.   It's less busy.

Está menos contaminado.   It's less polluted.

Soy muy deportista.   I'm very sporty.

Aiming higher

Use verb forms like me gustaba (I used to like) and me gustaría (I would like) to show variety in your use of language

Making comparisons   Grammar page 88

Use the comparative to compare two places / holidays to identify differences and similarities.

más	+ adjective + que = more ... than
menos	+ adjective + que = less ... than
tan	+ adjective + como = as ... as

Madrid es menos interesante que Barcelona.

Madrid is less interesting than Barcelona.

Las vacaciones con aventuras son más emocionantes que ir a la costa.
Adventure holidays are more exciting than going to the coast.

Worked example SPEAKING

¿Adónde prefieres ir de vacaciones?

Prefiero ir a la costa de Escocia, a pescar. Es más interesante que tomar el sol. Antes me gustaba ir a la playa pero hoy en día prefiero descansar y por eso me encantan las vacaciones más tranquilas.

AIMING HIGHER
Siempre me gusta mucho ir a la montaña, a Italia, a esquiar. Es más impresionante que nadar en el mar o en la piscina. Antes me gustaba ir a la playa pero hoy en día soy más deportista y por eso me fascinan las vacaciones de aventura. En el futuro me encantaría volver al extranjero.

The accurate use of the **imperfect** (me gustaba) and the comparative (**es más interesante**) shows the ability to produce longer, fluent sentences with ease. The connective **y por eso** is also an impressive inclusion.

Using opinion verbs in three different tenses (**me fascinan, me gustaba, me encantaría**) shows a confident use of more complex structures.

Now try this SPEAKING

Answer the question in Spanish. Aim to speak for at least a minute and a half.
¿Adónde vas de vacaciones?
- Say what kind of holiday you prefer.
- Compare it to other types of holiday.
- Include details of previous holidays.
- Say where you would like to go in the future.

Holiday accommodation

Use this page to talk more about your holidays and express your holiday preferences.

El alojamiento

Me quedo / Alojo en …	I stay in …
un camping	a campsite
un hotel de cinco estrellas	a five-star hotel
un albergue juvenil	a youth hostel
una pensión	a guest house
alquilar	to hire, rent
una caravana	a caravan
un piso alquilado	a rented flat
una casa	a house
nuestro apartamento en Francia	our flat in France
Prefiero quedarme en un hotel.	I prefer staying in a hotel.

Using me gusta(n) and me encanta(n)

Grammar page 103

Me gusta (I like) literally translates as 'it pleases me'. The thing that does the pleasing (i.e. the thing I like) is the subject. If this subject is plural, use me gustan. Me encanta behaves in the same way.

Me gusta dormir al aire libre.
I like sleeping outdoors.

Me encanta alquilar un apartamento.
I love renting a flat.

No me gusta quedarme en un camping.
I don't like staying on a campsite.

Aiming higher

Using quedarse as well as alojarse in the PRETERITE and FUTURE will improve your range of language marks.

me quedé / me alojé	I stayed
me quedaré / me alojaré	I will stay

me gusta ♥
me gusta mucho ♥ ♥
me encanta ♥ ♥ ♥

Worked example

 SPEAKING

¿Dónde prefieres alojarte?

Normalmente me gustan los hoteles porque son cómodos y bonitos. A veces prefiero un piso alquilado porque es más fácil y más barato.

AIMING HIGHER

Recientemente, me he quedado en un camping sencillo, pero el año pasado me alojé en un gran hotel precioso de cinco estrellas. En el hotel había bicicletas disponibles y visitamos la famosa plaza de toros. Pienso que el año que viene iré a Madrid para quedarme en un parador de lujo.

Speaking strategies

- Use CONNECTIVES to combine two short sentences: y (and) and pero (but) are the simplest.
- ADJECTIVES make your speaking and writing much more interesting: (precioso beautiful, de lujo luxury, sencillo simple), etc. Try to avoid over-using aburrido, interesante, importante, etc.
- Always show off your TENSES! Think PPF (present, past, future).

Now try this

 SPEAKING

Answer the question in Spanish. Aim to talk for at least one minute.
¿Adónde vas de vacaciones?

Booking accommodation

The language for booking accommodation here may crop up in listening and reading exams.

Reservar habitaciones

Quisiera reservar …	I'd like to reserve …
Pensamos quedarnos …	We are thinking of staying …
para una semana	one week
para la noche	for the night
desde el 6 hasta el 9 de enero	from 6 to 9 January
por la tarde	in the afternoon / evening
Somos cuatro.	There are four of us.
Vamos a llegar a …	We are going to arrive at …
Gracias por su ayuda	Thanks for your help
¿Cuánto cuesta?	How much does it cost?
con balcón	with a balcony
con aire acondicionado	with air conditioning

Using para and por

> Grammar page 104

POR – cause
Gracias por su ayuda. Thanks for your help.
POR – expressing rates
Son 50 euros por noche. It's 50 euros per night.
PARA – purpose
Voy a utilizar mi tarjeta de crédito para pagar el hotel. I'm going to use my credit card to pay the hotel.
PARA – period of time in the future
Quiero una habitación para una semana. I would like a room for a week.

con vistas al mar

Worked example

Read and choose the correct statement. Write the correct letter in the box.

Estimado señor,
Quisiera reservar una habitación para quince días para mi familia. Somos cinco personas y vamos a llegar el 15 de agosto por la tarde. La fecha de salida es el 29 de agosto. Quisiera, si es posible, habitaciones con balcón y vistas al mar. ¿Me puede decir el precio total?
Atentamente.
Ian Jones

A Ian wants a room for two weeks.
B Ian wants a room for five nights. [A]

Reading strategies

Make sure you do not neglect cross topic vocabulary when you are revising. Numbers, dates, opinions and negatives etc. can be just as important as actual hotel vocabulary.

Don't be put off by the formal style of this text or by the use of the **usted** form of the verb (**puede**). Remember, the **usted** endings of the verbs are the same as for the 'he / she' part of the verb.

Now try this

Which **three** of the following statements are true? Write the **three** correct letters in the boxes.

A Ian wants a room five people.
B Ian wants two single rooms.
C He does not want a balcony.

D He would prefer a sea view.
E He arrives on the 29th August.
F The reservation is for five people.

☐   ☐   ☐

Had a look ☐ Nearly there ☐ Nailed it! ☐

Staying in a hotel

Be prepared to talk in detail about where you stay on holiday.

En un hotel

Quisiera reservar ...	I'd like to reserve ...
una habitación individual / doble	a single /double room
sin baño	without a bathroom
con ducha / balcón	with a shower / balcony
¿Para cuántas noches?	For how many nights?
para siete noches	for seven nights
¿A qué hora sirven el desayuno / la cena?	What time is breakfast / dinner served?
¿Está incluido el desayuno?	Is breakfast included?
completo	full
la recepción	reception
la llave	key
el ascensor	lift
media pensión	half board
pensión completa	full board
conexión a internet	internet connection
con vistas al mar / a la piscina / a las montañas with a sea / pool / mountain view	

Revising numbers

Grammar page 107

You can never review numbers too often! Here are a few ideas:

- LOOK at the numbers on page 107. Can you identify any patterns that will help you remember them?
  - 16 to 19 are dieci + 6, dieci + 7, etc.
  - 31, 41, 51, etc. are always y uno (but 21 is different)
  - tres / trece / treinta (3 / 13 / 30)
- PLAY BINGO with friends. Agree on 12 numbers you all find difficult to distinguish (e.g. cinco/quince, ocho/ ochenta). One person is the caller; the others choose and write four of the numbers each. The caller reads out the numbers in random order until one of you has checked them all off – Bingo!
- PRACTISE numbers on your own: count in twos, in threes, in fives. Count backwards!

Worked example

 LISTENING 31 target E-F

Listen and write the correct letter in the box.
What kind of room does the man want?

A   B   C

B

- Hotel Luna. ¿Dígame?
- Quisiera reservar una habitación individual con baño y con vistas a las montañas.

EXAM ALERT!

Numbers often make an appearance in listening texts somewhere. Don't muddle similar sounding numbers: **quince** (15) with **cinco** (5) or **sesenta** (60) with **setenta** (70)

Students have struggled with exam questions similar to this – **be prepared!**

Work out which numbers you're going to listen for. That will help you identify the tricky ones.

Now try this

 LISTENING 32 target E-F

Listen to the whole recording and write the correct letter in each box.

1 How many nights does he want the room for?
   A 10 nights   B 2 nights   C 12 nights
   ☐

2 How much does it cost?
   A 360 €   B 370 €   C 270 €
   ☐

Staying on a campsite

Learn the camping vocabulary here to help you understand a reading text on rules and regulations.

En un camping

| una tienda | una caravana | los servicios | el parque infantil |

| las duchas | un saco de dormir | las canchas de tenis | los árboles |

las normas / las reglas	the rules
libre	available
hacer fuego	to light a fire
hacer una barbacoa	to have a barbecue
No se permite hacer ruido.	Being noisy is not allowed.
No se permiten animales.	Animals are not allowed.
Es obligatorio ...	It is compulsory ...

Using different verbs

To make your writing and speaking more varied, don't just use different tenses – use different verbs too. Make lists in diagrams like this:

ir — to go
llegar — to arrive
conducir — to drive
entrar — to enter
caminar — to walk
salir — to leave
pasar por — to pass by, go through
dejar — to leave
volver — to return
venir — to come
visitar — to visit

VERBS OF MOVEMENT

Note: Use **se permite** if it refers to a single thing, but **se permiten** if it refers to more than one thing.

Worked example

 target C

Read the text. Which rules are for the campsite or for the youth hostel? Write **C** (campsite) or **Y** (youth hostel) or **C + Y** (campsite + youth hostel).

En el camping
El horario de silencio es de 01:00h a 07:00h y se prohíbe la circulación de vehículos.

No se permite hacer carreras con bicicletas.

Están prohibidos los juegos de pelota cerca de las tiendas.

No se debe tirar basura.

El volumen o sonido de los aparatos de televisión debe ser, durante todo el día, lo más bajo posible.

En el albergue juvenil
No se permite hacer ruido después de medianoche.

No se permite comer en los dormitorios.

Es obligatorio tener saco de dormir propio.

Es obligatorio utilizar los cubos de basura.

You cannot make any noise at 2am. C+Y

EXAM ALERT!

Students score well in tasks like this when they have a good knowledge of basic vocabulary items and use deductive reasoning. Remember to use your ability to think as well as your knowledge of Spanish!

Students have struggled with exam questions similar to this – **be prepared!** ResultsPlus

Use deductive reasoning to help you work out answers. For example, where are you more likely to find bedrooms? In a campsite or in a youth hostel?

Now try this

 target C

Read the text again and complete the activity. Write **C, Y** or **C + Y.**
1 You must have your own sleeping bag ☐
2 No eating allowed in the bedrooms ☐
3 Ball games are not allowed ☐
4 No littering allowed ☐

Holiday activities

Be prepared to talk about a wide range of activities you do on holiday.

Las actividades de vacaciones

¿Qué haces normalmente cuando estás de vacaciones?

What do you normally do on holiday?

Voy ...	I go ...
con mi familia	with my family
con mis amigos	with my friends
Descanso / Me relajo.	I relax.
Me baño en el mar.	I swim in the sea.
Voy a discotecas.	I go to discos.
Monto en bicicleta.	I ride my bike.
Saco fotos.	I take photos.
Hago surfing.	I go surfing.
Compro recuerdos.	I buy souvenirs.
Hago esquí.	I ski.
Pinto y dibujo.	I paint and I draw.
Me bronceo.	I sunbathe.

Learning vocabulary

- Make yourself FLASHCARDS to help memorise vocabulary – Spanish on one side and English (or a picture) on the other.
- Write NOTECARDS to help you prepare for assessments – write key words and phrases, structures and verb forms under topic headings.

Tomamos el sol.
We sunbathe.

Worked example

¿Qué haces normalmente cuando estás de vacaciones?

Voy a Portugal con mis amigos porque es divertido y siempre hago surfing.

AIMING HIGHER Normalmente voy a Europa con mis hermanas. Es genial porque vamos a las discotecas. Nunca voy de vacaciones con mis padres porque me fastidian. Mis padres quieren que vayamos con ellos pero sé que es más entretenido estar con mis hermanas.

Speaking strategies

- Students who use a lot of words which are the same in English will only do well if they PRONOUNCE them in the correct Spanish way.
- Make sure you've learned a GOOD RANGE of vocabulary – filling a presentation with English words is not a good idea.

Review the **present tense** (see page 91) to prepare yourself for this topic. Don't just revise 'I' forms – be ready to talk about what your friends and family do on holiday, too, and what you do together.

Now try this

Answer this question. Aim to talk for a minute.

¿Qué haces normalmente cuando estás de vacaciones?

Holiday preferences

This page will help you express your opinions in lots of different ways.

Prefiero las vacaciones ...

Prefiero las vacaciones en la playa con amigos.
I prefer holidays on the beach with friends.

Mis vacaciones ideales serían en el Caribe.
My ideal holiday would be in the Caribbean.

Es maravilloso conocer una ciudad y perderme por los barrios antiguos.
It's wonderful getting to know a city and losing myself in the old town.

Siempre he querido visitar Australia.
I have always wanted to visit Australia.

Es fantástico descansar sin pensar en el instituto.
It's fantastic to rest without thinking about school.

No me gusta ir de vacaciones con mis padres.
I don't like going on holiday with my parents.

Me da asco hacer camping.
I hate going camping.

Odio los sitios arruinados por el turismo descontrolado.
I hate places ruined by uncontrolled tourism.

Me da vergüenza el comportamiento de los británicos.
The behaviour of British holidaymakers makes me ashamed.

Odio el sol porque siempre me pongo rojo.
I hate the sun as it always makes me red.

Me aburren los museos y la historia.
Museums and history bore me.

Worked example

Talk about your preferred holiday destination.

Mis vacaciones ideales serían en España. Primero, diría que las vacaciones en España sin padres son fenomenales pero ellos pagan por todo así que con padres no están tan mal.

- This question allows use of the **conditional** to say what your favourite type of holiday **would** be.
- A **time phrase** (primero) and a **connective** (pero) make this answer more sophisticated.

AIMING HIGHER

Mis vacaciones ideales serían en América Latina, en un país como México. Primero, diría que las vacaciones al extranjero sin padres son muy emocionantes. Sin embargo, son los padres quienes pagan por todo así que ¡viajar con padres no será tan mal! He visitado muchos lugares en el mundo y es maravilloso conocer culturas distintas a la mía.

The use of both the **perfect** he visitado (I have visited) and **la mía** (mine) makes for a more complex answer.

Aiming higher

Try to work in MORE COMPLEX language.

Mis padres siempre quieren que vaya con ellos.
My parents always want me to go with them.

Si pudiera, iría a Ibiza para ir a las discotecas.
If I could, I'd go to Ibiza to go to nightclubs.

Now try this

Write about your preferred holiday destination. Write at least 100 words.

- Refer to different options you have thought about, considering pros and cons.
- Write about holidays you have already had, including opinions.

Future holiday plans

Make sure you know the future tense to be able to talk about holiday plans.

Vacaciones futuras

Iré ...	I will go ...
a la costa	to the coast
a la montaña	to the mountains
a la playa	to the beach
al campo	to the country
Descansaré.	I will rest.
Nadaré.	I will swim.
Haré yoga.	I will do yoga.
Iré a clases de baile.	I will go to dance classes.
Daré una vuelta en bicicleta.	I will go on a cycling tour.
Veré lugares de interés.	I will see places of interest.
Montaré a caballo.	I will go horseriding.
Patinaré.	I will go skating.
Iré a esquiaré.	I will go skiing.
Haré alpinismo.	I will go climbing.
Haré vela.	I will go sailing.
Nos quedaremos en un hotel.	We will stay in a hotel.

Future tense

Grammar page 97

To form the future tense of most verbs, add the following endings to the infinitive:

	ir – to go
I will go	iré
you will go	irás
he / she will go	irá
we will go	iremos
you will go	iréis
they will go	irán

¿Adónde irás de vacaciones el año que viene?

Where will you go on holiday next year?

Iré a Grecia y daré una vuelta en bicicleta.
I'll go to Greece and I'll go on a cycling tour.

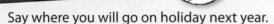

Worked example

WRITING

Say where you will go on holiday next year.

El año que viene, iré a esquiar en Francia con mi instituto. Va a ser genial.

Using the **future** and the **near future** shows variety of tense usage that can improve language knowledge marks.

AIMING HIGHER

Este año veré varios lugares de interés en Francia con un grupo de mi instituto. Creo que va a ser maravilloso. Nos quedaremos en un hotel cerca de las montañas. Iré con mi novio y creo que será perfecto porque serán nuestras primeras vacaciones juntos.

- Extending **opinions** by justifying them using **connectives** (**y, porque**) will help you aim higher.

- Also, use **interesting phrases** to show your grasp of a wider range of vocabulary, e.g **nuestras primeras vacaciones juntos** (our first holiday together).

Now try this

WRITING

Write about where you will go on holiday next year. Write at least eighty words.

Mention:

- the destination
- who you will go with and for how long
- what you will do
- what it will be like and why.

Holiday experiences

Past holidays is a popular topic in the exam. Make sure you've revised the appropriate verb forms.

Las vacaciones del año pasado

¿Adónde fuiste de vacaciones el año pasado?
Where did you go on holiday last year?

el verano pasado	last summer
hace dos años	two years ago
Fui...	I went ...
con mi familia	with my family
con mis amigos	with my friends
solo/a	alone
Me alojé ... / Me quedé ...	I stayed...
Viajé en ...	I travelled by...
Hice un intercambio.	I did an exchange.
Pasé una semana allí.	I spent one week there.

Hice un viaje escolar.
I went on a school trip.

Preterite tense

Grammar page 95

To form the preterite tense of regular verbs, replace the infinitive ending as follows:

	visitar – to visit	comer – to eat	salir – to go out
I	visité	comí	salí
you	visitaste	comiste	saliste
he / she	visitó	comió	salió
we	visitamos	comimos	salimos
you	visitasteis	comisteis	salisteis
they	visitaron	comieron	salieron

Useful verbs in the preterite for talking about holidays:

vi	I saw
bebí	I drank
hice	I did
tuve	I had
fue	it was

Worked example

 SPEAKING

¿Adónde fuiste de vacaciones el año pasado?

El verano pasado fui a Marruecos. Pasé dos semanas allí y fue una experiencia estupenda. Viajé en avión y el vuelo duró tres horas.

AIMING HIGHER

Durante las vacaciones pasadas mi familia y yo fuimos a Alemania. Pasamos dos semanas allí y fue una experiencia única. Viajamos en avión pero lo peor fue que el vuelo sólo duró dos horas así que la próxima vez, ¡me gustaría viajar a los Estados Unidos y poder ver muchas películas buenas durante el vuelo!

CONTROLLED ASSESSMENT

Your speaking assessment should last between four and six minutes. Students who speak for only three minutes do not do as well as other candidates. However, it is better to talk accurately and fluently for five minutes than to keep talking for six minutes and start to hesitate and make mistakes.

Including opinions will allow you to do better in your speaking assessment.
Lo peor fue ...   The worst thing was ...
Lo mejor fue ...   The best thing was ...

Now try this

 SPEAKING

Prepare your answer to the following question. Aim to talk for at least two minutes.
¿Adónde fuiste de vacaciones el año pasado?

Countries and nationalities

If you are writing from a female perspective, remember to use the feminine form for nationalities.

Países y nacionalidades

Soy de / Vivo en   I'm from / I live in

Countries		Nationalities
España		español / española
Inglaterra		inglés / inglesa
Escocia		escocés / escocesa
Gales		galés / galesa
Gran Bretaña		británico/a
Irlanda		irlandés / itlandesa
Grecia		griego/a
Francia		francés / francesa
Alemania		alemán / alemana
Estados Unidos		estadounidense

In Spanish, nationalities don't have a capital letter.

Talking about nationalities

Grammar page 86

Like other adjectives, adjectives of nationality agree.

	Singular	Plural
Nationalities ending -o:		
Masculine	griego	griegos
Feminine	griega	griegas
Nationalities ending in a consonant:		
Masculine	inglés	ingleses
Feminine	inglesa	inglesas

When you talk about people from a country, you always use the definite article.

Me gustan los españoles.
I like Spanish people.

Nationalities with an accent on the ending lose it in feminine and plural forms, e.g. escocés   escocesa   escoseses

Worked example

WRITING

Write about where you were born.

AIMING HIGHER

Nací en Irlanda, aunque vivo en Inglaterra porque mis padres trabajan aquí. Sin embargo, mi madre es estadounidense y nació en Nueva York, así que soy mitad irlandés, mitad estadounidense. Me gustan los ingleses. En el futuro viviré en Londres.

Aiming higher

✓ The use of THREE tenses (present, preterite and future) will help you achieve well for knowledge and range of language categories.

✓ Using CONNECTIVES and conjunctions makes your writing coherent and more interesting.

Now try this

WRITING

Write about where you were born. Aim to write 50 words.
- Say where you were born.
- Say where you live now.
- Say what nationality you and your parents are.

- Use the text above as a guide.
- Include **connectives** and a **range** of tenses.

My house

Make sure you know lots of house vocabulary to be able to talk about your home.

Mi casa

un aseo
una cocina
un cuarto de baño
un dormitorio / una habitación
un comedor
un jardín
un salón

Vivo en una casa adosada.
I live in a terraced house.

Vivo en una granja.
I live on a farm.

Alquilamos un piso en la planta baja.
We rent a flat on the ground floor.

Using the verb 'to be': ser and estar

Grammar page 93

Use ser to describe your house but estar to explain where it is located.

Está en ...	It's in / on ...
la costa	the coast
las montañas	the mountains
las afueras	the suburbs
Es ...	It's ...
bonito	pretty
antiguo / viejo	old
ruidoso	noisy

La casa está en el centro de la ciudad.
The house is in the city centre.

Mi piso es cómodo y moderno.
My flat is comfortable and modern.

Worked example

LISTENING 33 · target C

Listen and write the correct letter in the box.
Where does Carmen's family have a holiday home?

A 
B 
C 

C

Para las vacaciones, mis padres tienen una casa en la costa. *Carmen*

Remember to think about all the **possible words** which could represent each picture. Picture C could prompt **cerca de la playa** but also **en la costa**, which is the phrase Carmen uses.

Now try this

LISTENING 34 · target C

Listen to Carmen again. Write the correct letter in the boxes.

1 What is the holiday home like? ☐

A 
B 
C 

2 Where does Ramona sleep? ☐

A 
B 
C 

My room

Use the opinion expressions below to say what you think about your room.

Los muebles

el estante / la estantería
the shelf / shelves

el armario
the wardrobe /
cupboard

el estéreo
the music system

la silla
the chair

la ventana
the window

la alfombra
the rug

la cortina
the curtain

la moqueta
the carpet

la cama
the bed

el espejo   the mirror
la lámpara   the lamp
la librería   the bookcase
la papelera   the bin

Opinions

Try to avoid using simply **me gusta** or **no me gusta** to give your opinion.

Lo bueno es que…
The good thing is that …

Lo malo es que …
The bad thing is that …

Lo que más me gusta es que …
The thing I like best is that …

Lo que menos me gusta es que …
The thing I like least is that …

Opino que … / Pienso que …
I think that …

Worked example

¿Te gusta tu dormitorio?

Pienso que mi dormitorio es pequeño pero lo bueno es que tiene un estéreo y un ordenador. Mi cama está al lado de la ventana y tengo una lámpara amarilla. Es muy bonita.

AIMING HIGHER

Lo que menos me gusta de mi dormitorio es que lo tengo que compartir con mis dos hermanas pequeñas. Ayer mis hermanas no hicieron las camas y dejaron la ropa por todas partes. Ahora mi madre me ha dicho que no puedo salir esta noche porque debemos limpiar la habitación. No es justo y opino que mis hermanas deben hacerlo.

CONTROLLED ASSESSMENT

Examiners have commented that candidates do not do well when they try to memorise difficult phrases which they do not really understand properly. Make sure you understand what you are trying to say!

Use **opinions** and **adjectives** to make your answer more interesting.

To improve even more, use a **range of tenses** and try to include **complex structures** using subordinate clauses such as **ahora mi madre me ha dicho que no puedo salir esta noche porque debemos limpiar la habitación** (now my mother has said I can't go out tonight because we have to clean the room).

Now try this

You are being interviewed about your experience of a house-swap with a family from Spain. Prepare answers to the following. Aim to speak for 1 minute. You could include:

- what the holiday home in Spain is like.
- what you think could be improved.

Had a look ☐ Nearly there ☐ Nailed it! ☐

HOME AND ENVIRONMENT

Helping at home

There are not many cognates in helping at home vocabulary, so learn your words carefully.

Las tareas

Tengo que ...	I have to ...
Debo ...	I should / must ...
cortar el césped	mow the lawn
arreglar las cosas	tidy up
limpiar mi dormitorio	clean my room
limpiar el frigorífico	clean the fridge
poner / vaciar el lavaplatos	load / unload the dishwasher
poner / quitar la mesa	lay / clear the table
hacer la cama	make the bed
poner la ropa en la lavadora	put clothes in the washing machine
pasar la aspiradora	do the hoovering

The imperfect tense

Grammar page 96

Remember to use the imperfect when you describe what you used to do, as well as the following time phrases:

antes	before
a menudo	often
siempre	always
nunca	never
todos los días / cada día	every day

Antes cortaba el césped cada semana pero ahora lo hace mi hermano.
I used to mow the lawn every week but now my brother does it.

Worked example

Read the texts.

Elena
Me llevo bien con mis padres pero soy hija única y por eso tengo que ayudar mucho en casa. Lo odio. Siempre tengo que limpiar el microondas y la cocina de gas. Antes ponía la mesa cada noche pero ahora no comemos juntos porque mi madre trabaja hasta tarde.

Javier
Antes tenía una buena relación con mi padre pero ahora no, porque siempre dice que debo limpiar mi dormitorio. A menudo hago la cama. Mi hermana siempre ponía la ropa en la lavadora pero ahora tiene éxamenes y no tiene que hacer nada. No es justo.

Identify the people. Write **E** (Elena), **J** (Javier) or **E + J** (Elena + Javier).

Who has to do chores at home?

E + J

Answering *who* questions

- This is a common type of question in the reading paper. Knowing TIME EXPRESSIONS will help you identify tenses correctly.

- When comparing two texts, it is important to read them both thoroughly as you may need to DEDUCE information from the texts.

In Elena's text she specifically mentions helping at home (**tengo que ayudar mucho**). However, you have to **deduce** this from Javier writing that his Dad tells him that he should clean his room and that he often makes the bed (**a menudo hago la cama**).

Now try this

Read the text again and identify the people. Write **E** (Elena), **J** (Javier) or **E + J** (Elena + Javier).

1 Who does not get on well with with their father? ☐
2 Who has a family member who used to help more with the chores? ☐
3 Who has stopped doing one of their chores? ☐

My neighbourhood

The key to this topic is learning opinions and adjectives. If you know this language well, it will help you in your listening exam.

Mi barrio

Mi barrio es ruidoso.	My neighbourhood is noisy.
una ciudad histórica	a historic city
un pueblo conocido	a well-known village
una provincia bonita	a beautiful province / area
una región tranquila	a quiet region
un bosque	a wood
el campo	the countryside
el río	the river
las flores	flowers
la sierra	the mountain range
la zona	the area / zone
industrial	industrial
residencial	residential
mudarse (de casa)	to move house
construir	to build

Fue construido durante los años setenta.
It was built during the seventies.

Connectives

Use connectives to help you structure your opinions.

además	also, as well
por un lado … por otro lado …	on the one hand … on the other hand …
por una parte … por otra parte …	on one side… on the other side …
en realidad	actually / in fact
aparte de	apart from
a pesar de esto	in spite of this
es decir	that is to say / I mean
sin duda	without a doubt

Me parece una región histórica con muchos edificios impresionantes y sin duda, es un lugar tranquilo.
It seems like a historic region with many impressive buildings and it is, without doubt, a peaceful area.

Worked example

Listen and write **P** (positive), **N** (negative) or **P + N** (positive and negative).

What does Lalo think of his town?
☐ N

– ¿Qué piensas de nuestra ciudad, Lalo?

– La zona junto al castillo me parece sucia y un poco ruidosa. También hay otros barrios aquí que son francamente aburridos.

EXAM ALERT!

Pupils often miss out on achieving a high grade by not identifying opinions correctly. Just because you hear a **no** don't assume it's a negative opinion. e.g. **No me gustaría vivir en otro lugar** (I wouldn't like to live anywhere else) is a positive opinion!

Students have struggled with exam questions similar to this – **be prepared!**

Now try this

Listen to the rest of the recording and complete the activity. Write **P** (positive), **N** (negative) or **P + N** (positive and negative)

1 Cristina ☐   2 Matías ☐

Places in town

You need to know places in town and prepositions to give and understand directions.

En la ciudad

el centro comercial	shopping centre
la peluquería	hairdresser
el mercado	market
correos	post office
el ayuntamiento	town hall
la comisaría	police station
el polideportivo	sports centre
la piscina	swimming pool
el colegio / el instituto	school
la pista de hielo	ice rink
la biblioteca	library
el teatro	theatre

Saying 'I go' in different tenses

voy	I go (present)
fui	I went (preterite)
iba	I used to go / was going (imperfect)
iré	I will go (future)
he ido	I have been (perfect)

Prepositions

Use prepositions to describe location.
Note that de + el changes to del.

Está …

delante de   detrás de

al lado de   entre

cerca de	near
lejos de	far from
enfrente de	opposite-hand side
a mano derecha	on the right-hand side
a mano izquierda	on the left-hand side
en la esquina	on the corner
a 10 minutos	10 minutes away

Está delante del cine.
It's in front of the cinema.

Worked example LISTENING 37 target A-B

Listen and answer the question.
Where did Luisa go yesterday and why?

She went to the library to study for the exam.

– ¡Hola, Luisa! ¿Dónde fuiste?
– Anteayer fui a la peluquería porque estaba harta de tener el pelo largo. Luego ayer, iba a ir a las tiendas pero al final fui a la biblioteca para estudiar para el examen.

Listening strategies

- Remember to listen all the way to the END of what someone says. If you thought you'd got the answer from the first part (a las tiendas), you'd be wrong!

- Listen carefully to VERBS to try and work out the correct tense (iba a ir – 'I was going to go'). Also listen for other CLUE WORDS, e.g. al final, which here indicates a change of plan.

Now try this LISTENING 38 target A-B

Listen to the whole recording and answer the questions.

1 Where did Luisa go to do this and why?
2 Where does Ignacio have to go later and at what time?

At the tourist office

You need to know the vocabulary for tourist attractions. Learn the genders too!

En la oficina de turismo

¿Tiene...?   Do you have...?

un mapa de la región   a map of the region

una lista de hoteles / albergues de juventud
a list of hotels / youth hostels

un folleto de excursiones
a brochure about trips

un horario de trenes / autobuses
a train / bus timetable

¿A qué hora abre / cierra el museo?
What time does the museum open / close?

¿Qué hay de interés en Calella?
What is there of interest in Calella?

Quisiera información sobre ...
I'd like information on ...

Hay ...
There is / There are ...

Es posible ...
It's possible ...

Si yo fuera usted, visitaría ...
If I were you, I would visit ...

Question words

Grammar page 105

¿Dónde?	Where?
¿Adónde?	Where to?
¿Cuánto?	How much?
¿Cuándo? / ¿A qué hora?	When?
¿Qué?	What?
¿Cómo?	How?
¿Cuál?	Which?

Attractions in a town

playas bonitas	beautiful beaches
museos interesantes	interesting museums
la comida rica	tasty food
una zona peatonal	a pedestrian zone

Los jardines son bonitos. The gardens are beautiful.

Worked example

READING / target D

Read about Palafrugell, a town in Spain.

What number do you click on to find out about shopping? Write the correct number in the box. [4]

Para más información sobre Palafrugell, hacer 'clic' en uno de estos números:

1 Transporte   4 Tiendas
2 Alojamiento   5 Clima
3 Fiestas   6 Cultura

Reading strategies

• Read all the items at least TWICE and think about what they mean in English.

• Don't panic if there is a word you do NOT UNDERSTAND. For example, you may not remember that alojamiento means accommodation but in this case you do not need to know this to get the correct answer.

Now try this

READING / target D

What number do you click on to find out about ...?

1 museums ☐   2 weather ☐   3 how to travel to Palafrugell ☐

Things to do in town

This page gives more town vocabulary to help with listening and reading tasks.

Actividades en la ciudad

¿Qué se puede hacer en tu ciudad?
What can you do in your town?

En (Bilbao) se puede ...
In (Bilbao) you can ...

visitar los museos	visit museums
ir a una galería de arte	go to an art gallery
ir a la mezquita	go to the mosque
ir a la piscina	go to the swimming pool
jugar en los parques	play in the parks
conocer la cultura	experience the culture
ver un espectáculo de flamenco	see a flamenco show
ver el puerto	see the port
ver plazas y puentes	see squares and bridges

Se puede ir a la catedral.

Using se puede to say what you can do

Se puede is an impersonal verb used to talk about what people in general can do. It is followed by the infinitive.

Se puede visitar un parque temático.
You can visit a theme park.

If you are talking about more than one activity, use se pueden:

Se pueden practicar deportes.
You can do sports.

Worked example

What can you do in your town?

> En mi ciudad se puede visitar el museo y así se conoce la cultura. También se puede ver plazas bonitas y jugar en los parques.

AIMING HIGHER

> Mi ciudad tiene un poco de todo. Por ejemplo, se puede pasear por el barrio antiguo donde a veces se puede disfrutar de un espectáculo de música tradicional. A mi modo de ver, la música es importante para nosotros porque forma parte de nuestro patrimonio cultural.

Aiming higher

If you want a higher grade, try to include the following features:

✓ a connective (así, porque, por ejemplo, etc.) to make a complex sentence

✓ opinion phrases (en mi opinión, a mi modo de ver)

✓ less common verbs such as pasear and disfrutar de (to show a wider range of vocabulary)

✓ more detail (make sure it's relevant!)

Now try this

Remember to use the Aiming higher advice!

Write a piece for a Spanish blog about interesting places to visit in other countries.
Write at least 100 words about where you live and why it's a great place to visit!

Signs around town

Town signs often crop up in reading tasks – make sure you know them.

Las señales

la entrada
entrance

la salida
exit

la estación de servicio
petrol station

la estación de autobuses
bus station

la piscina
swimming pool

el aparcamiento
car park

el cajero
cashpoint

el centro de la ciudad
town centre

los servicios
toilets

el puente
bridge

abierto
open

cerrado
closed

Understanding instructions

Grammar page 100

These expressions all feature in town signs. You can also use them to explain what people in general aren't allowed to do and what's compulsory.

Note that they are all followed by an INFINITIVE.

No se permite …   You are not allowed …

Está prohibido …   It is forbidden …

No se debe …   You shouldn't …

Tiene que …   You have to …

No se permite fumar.
You are not allowed to smoke.

Está prohibido aparcar.
It is forbidden to park.

Worked example

Signs in a town

A La estación de autobuses

B Aparcamiento

C Parque infantil

D Piscina

E Cajero

F La estación de servicio

Look for any words that look like the English, e.g. **estación** – station. Words that end in 'tion' in English often correspond to Spanish words ending in **ción**.

Where should they go? Write the correct letter in the boxes

1 I need to take money out. ☐ E

Now try this

Look at the signs again and complete the activity. Where should they go?

1 My motorbike needs petrol. ☐

2 We want to go swimming. ☐

3 She's going shopping and needs to park her car. ☐

Where I live

Use this page to talk about the pros and cons of where you live.

Mi barrio

Lo bueno es que ...	The good thing is that ...
Es limpio.	It's clean.
Es tranquilo.	It's peaceful.
Hay vistas bonitas.	There are beautiful views.
La gente es generosa.	The people are kind.
Hay mucho que hacer.	There's lots to do.
Hay muchas diversiones para los jóvenes.	
There are lots of attractions for young people.	
Hay mucha industria.	
There is a lot of industry.	
Lo malo es que ...	The bad thing is that ...
Hay contaminación.	There's pollution.
Es ruidoso.	It's noisy.
Es peligroso.	It's dangerous
Hay mucho turismo.	There's a lot of tourism.
Hay demasiado tráfico.	There's too much traffic.
La vivienda es cara.	Housing is expensive.

lo + adjective

Use lo + adjective to refer to an abstract idea.

lo bueno	the good thing
lo malo	the bad thing
lo aburrido	the boring thing
lo interesante	the interesting thing

There is also a superlative form:

Lo más interesante es que hay lagos bonitos. The most interesting thing is the beautiful lakes.

Aiming higher

Using haber in three tenses will help you give a good answer.

Hay	There is / are (present tense)
Había	There used to be / there was (imperfect past)
Habrá	There will be (future)

Worked example SPEAKING

¿Qué piensas de tu pueblo?

> Lo que más me gusta de mi pueblo es que es tranquilo y hay muchas playas bonitas. Antes había mucho turismo y mucha contaminación.

AIMING HIGHER

> Me encanta mi pueblo porque hay mucho que hacer. Vivo aquí desde hace once años. Lo que más me gusta de mi pueblo es que es tranquilo y hay muchas playas bonitas. Antes había mucho turismo y mucha contaminación. En el futuro, habrá muchas diversiones para los jóvenes.

CONTROLLED ASSESSMENT

Remember that you will be asked an unpredictable question during your speaking task. You must answer the question using a verb otherwise you will not pass that element of the test. An unpredictable question for this context could be **¿Piensas que tu (barrio/ciudad) tiene bastante para los jóvenes?**.

As well as using **haber** in **three tenses** (hay, había, habrá), this version uses extended sequences of speech using more complex structures (**Lo que más me gusta**) and verb tenses (**había, habrá**) improve the answer further.

Now try this SPEAKING

Answer this question. Aim to talk for at least one minute. **¿Qué piensas de tu pueblo?**

Remember to include **reasons** and **opinions**.

Town description

This page will help you describe your town and talk about what things you would change there.

Descripción de mi ciudad

Mi ciudad se llama …   My town is called …

Está en el norte / este / sur / oeste de Inglaterra.
It is in the north / east / south / west of England.

Hay doce mil habitantes.
There are 12,000 inhabitants.

En mi ciudad hay muchos turistas.
In my town there are lots of tourists.

una buena red de transporte público
a good public transport network

muchos lugares de ocio   lots of leisure areas

mucha contaminación   lots of pollution

muchos árboles   lots of trees

una falta de instalaciones   a lack of facilities

En mi ciudad hay muchos espacios verdes.
In my town there are lots of green spaces.

Conditional

Grammar page 98

You use the conditional to talk about what you WOULD do. To form it, add the following endings to the infinitive. Use the same endings for all infinitives.

	hablar – to speak
I	hablaría
you	hablarías
he / she	hablaría
we	hablaríamos
you	hablaríais
they	hablarían

Construiría …   I would build …
Podría …   I would be able to …
Habría …   There would be …
Mejoraría …   I would improve …

Worked example

LISTENING 39   *target A*

Listen to Pedro. Complete the table.

Name	Problem mentioned	Action required	When
Pedro	Not enough housing	Build blocks of flats	As soon as possible

Vivo en Valencia, una ciudad que tiene casi ochocientos mil habitantes y muy pocas casas. La vivienda es insuficiente. El gobierno debe construir más bloques de pisos lo más pronto posible.

Listening strategies

- ALWAYS complete the table in English if the headings are in English. Be precise and concise.
- NEVER leave a blank. If after the second listening you are still unsure, make an educated guess.

Look at the table. What do you need to listen out for?

- **Key words** for possible problems in a town (vivienda, contaminación, fábricas, etc.)
- **Time references** (pronto, el año que viene, dentro de 5 años, etc)
- **Verbs** in the future tense or future phrases

Now try this

 LISTENING 40   *target A*

Listen to Iván and complete the table.

Name	Problem mentioned	Action required	When
Iván			

Weather

Try to add a weather phrase in your writing and speaking assessments. Use a range of tenses!

El clima / El tiempo

Llueve / Está lloviendo. Nieva / Está nevando.

Hace sol.   Hay niebla.

Hace calor.   Hace frío.

Hace viento.	It's windy.
el pronóstico del tiempo	weather forecast
el clima	the climate
Hace mal tiempo.	It's bad weather.
Hace buen tiempo.	It's good weather.
Está nublado.	It's cloudy.
Hay tormenta / chubascos.	It's stormy.
seco	dry
mojado	wet

Different tenses

Understanding the weather in different tenses is a higher-level skill.

Expressions with hacer	
Hacía calor.	It was hot.
Hará frío.	It will be cold.
Expressions with estar	
Estaba nublado.	It was cloudy.
Estará soleado.	It will be sunny.
Expressions with haber	
Había niebla.	It was foggy.
Habrá tormenta.	It will be stormy.
nevar (to snow) and llover (to rain)	
Nevaba.	It was snowing.
Llovía.	It was raining.
Nevará / lloverá.	It will snow / rain.

Look out for time phrases as clues to the tense.

ayer	yesterday
hoy	today
mañana	tomorrow

Worked example

 LISTENING 41   target C

Listen and write the correct letter in the box.
The forecast for Bilbao today is

A sun   **B** rain   **C** snow

☐ A

Bilbao, sábado 12 de marzo. Ayer llovía pero hoy hace sol. Mañana nevará.

The key word to listen out for here is **hoy** (today).

EXAM ALERT!

Some candidates make errors because they haven't learned key vocabulary like time expressions. Make sure you know your dates, numbers and time references.

Students have struggled with exam questions similar to this – **be prepared!**

Now try this

 LISTENING 42   target C

Listen to the whole recording and write the correct letter in the boxes.

1 Tomorrow it will snow in   **A** Seville   **B** Bilbao   **C** both cities ☐

2 In Seville yesterday it was   **A** windy   **B** cold   **C** foggy ☐

3 In Seville now it is   **A** hot   **B** stormy   **C** cold ☐

It will also help you if you recognise the tenses used. Make sure you know **hacer, estar** and **haber** in the imperfect, present and future tenses.

Celebrations at home

Make sure you review the language for celebrations. Be prepared to talk about how you and your family celebrate.

¡Felicidades!

la fiesta de cumpleaños	birthday party
la Navidad	Christmas
la Nochebuena	Christmas Eve
la Nochevieja	New Year's Eve
el Año Nuevo	New Year
Papa Noël	Father Christmas
el Día de Reyes	Epiphany (6th January)
la Semana Santa	Easter
la boda	wedding
el aniversario	anniversary

¡Feliz Navidad!
Happy Christmas

¡Feliz cumpleaños!
Happy birthday

¡Felices Pascuas!
Happy Easter

¡Feliz Año Nuevo!
Happy New Year

Using different tenses

Present

Normalmente, celebramos …
Normally, we celebrate …
Vienen …
nuestros amigos / abuelos / primos, etc.
Our friends / grandparents, etc. come.

Preterite

Invité a …	I invited …
Comimos …	We ate …
Fue (genial)!	It was (great)!

Imperfect

Antes íbamos a …	We used to go to …
Había mucha gente.	There were a lot of people.

Future

Iremos a …	We will go to …
Será (fantástico).	It will be (fantastic).

Worked example

Write about your celebrations at home.

> Cumplí quince años el fin de semana pasado. Por la tarde fui al cine con mis mejores amigos y por la noche celebramos una fiesta en casa. Invité a diez amigos y mis primos vinieron también. Lo pasé fenomenal.

Here the preterite tense has been used successfully (**cumplí, fui, invité, vinieron,** etc.). The student has also included an opinion (**lo pasé fenomenal**).

AIMING HIGHER

> Celebramos siempre la Semana Santa, la Navidad y la Nochevieja en casa con toda la familia. Sin embargo, la Navidad me parece el día más emocionante del año porque siempre lo celebramos con mucha comida, varios regalos y, ¡una visita de Papa Noël! Hace dos años estuvimos en España y me encantó ver cómo se celebra el Día de Reyes pero este año nos quedaremos en casa.

This has a greater variety of vocabulary and present, preterite and future tenses (**celebramos, estuvimos, nos quedaremos**). Interesting and complex structures also raise the level of the description (**la Navidad me parece …, me encantó ver cómo se celebra …**).

Now try this

Write a short article about your celebrations at home. Aim to write 100 words. Include:

- a description of a recent celebration you've had at home
- something you'd like to do to celebrate your next birthday.

Directions

Learn the key vocabulary here to understand amd give directions.

Las direcciones

¿Dónde está ...?   Where is ...?

¿Por dónde se va a ...? How do you get to ...?

Tuerza / Doble a la derecha.

Tuerza / Doble a la izquierda.

Siga todo recto.

Tome la primera calle a la izquierda.

Tome la segunda calle a la derecha.

Pase el puente.

Pase los semáforos.

Giving instructions

Grammar page 100

Use the IMPERATIVE to give instructions. There are two forms, depending on whether you are talking to a friend (informal) or a stranger (formal).

informal (friend)	formal (stranger)	
sigue	siga	follow
tuerce	tuerza	turn
dobla	doble	turn
cruza	cruce	cross
toma	tome	take

la tercera calle   the third road

Doble la esquina. Turn the corner.

Cruce la plaza.   Cross the square.

Worked example

 43 target D

Listen and complete the grid.

Place	Directions given
Church	Straight on, past the traffic lights

Para ir a la iglesia, siga todo recto y luego pase los semáforos.

Remember that straight on **todo recto** and right **derecha** can sound quite similar in a listening, so you need to listen for the verb carefully: **siga todo recto** and **tuerza a la derecha**.

Listening strategies

- You can ANTICIPATE the words you will need to listen for from the grid headings. Don't forget to be precise with the English you use. For example, for doble a la derecha you would need to write 'turn right' and not just 'right'.

- Listen out for key direction VERBS. Here it doesn't matter if they're formal or informal – you just need to recognise the verb.

Now try this

 44   target D

Listen and complete the grid.

Place	Directions given

Transport

Use this vocabulary to understand and talk about how people get around.

El transporte

en coche   en tren   en barco   en metro   en moto

en autobús   en autocar   en bicicleta   en avión   a pie

Es …	It's …
limpio	clean
sucio	dirty
cómodo	comfortable
incómodo	uncomfortable
lento	slow
rápido	fast
barato	cheap
caro	expensive

mejor para el medio ambiente
better for the environment

Viajo en avión.
I travel by plane.

Prefiero coger el autobús.
I prefer to catch the bus.

Odio ir andando.
I hate walking.

Note **cojo** –
I catch.
Cojo el autobús.

Worked example

 target **B**

Raúl considers the advantages and disadvantages of various modes of transport.

What does he mention for each?

Write **A** (advantage only), **D** (disadvantage only) or **A + D** (advantage and disadvantage).

Los barcos son bastante cómodos; sin embargo salen muy caros para viajar a otros países y hay que reservar con anticipación.

Boat	A + D

- When looking for advantages and disadvantages, make sure that you pay attention to the **conjunctions** and **connectives** as they give you valuable clues.

- Here, Raúl says **sin embargo** (nevertheless) which suggests he will list a disadvantage too, which he does!

Now try this

target **B**

Read these texts and write **A**, **D** or **A + D** for each one.

Estoy harto de viajar en coche porque causa mucho daño al medio ambiente. También la gasolina es cara y el tráfico es horroroso.

Los autocares son un medio de transporte bastante barato y son mejor para el medio ambiente. Por otra parte, los viajes en autocar duran mucho tiempo y los asientos son incómodos.

car ☐   coach ☐

At the train station

As well as revising ticket vocabulary, make sure you know your numbers for times and prices.

Comprar billetes

Quiero dos billetes para ...
I would like two tickets to ...

¿A qué hora sale / llega?
What time does it depart / arrive?

¿Cuánto tiempo dura el viaje?
How long does the journey take?

un billete de ida	a single ticket
un billete de ida y vuelta	a return ticket
para hoy / mañana	for today / tomorrow
de primera clase	first class
Es directo.	It's direct.
el andén	the platform
¿Cuánto cuesta?	How much does it cost?
Dura ...	It takes ...
el próximo tren	the next train
el último tren	the last train
acabar de llegar	to have just arrived
acabar de salir	to have just left

The 24-hour clock

The 24-hour clock is often used to talk about travel times.

las nueve treinta	las doce cuarenta y cinco	las dieciséis quince

las diecinueve cero cinco	las veinte cuarenta	las veintitrés

El tren llega a las veinte treinta.
The train arrives at 20.30.

El tren sale a las diez quince.
The train leaves at 10.15.

Worked example target D

Listen and write the correct letter in the boxes.

The man wants to buy

A a single ticket
B a ticket to Valencia
C a ticket for tomorrow

☐ A

Quiero un billete de ida a Sevilla para hoy.

- Be prepared for listening questions which contain numbers or prices. Be careful with similar sounding numbers like **seis**, **siete**, **sesenta** and **setenta** (6, 7, 60 and 70).

- Remember that if you are listening for a price which contains cents as well as euros you may not necessarily hear the word **céntimo**.

- 5,60 = cinco euros con sesenta céntimos or cinco euros con sesenta or just cinco con sesenta.

Now try this target D

Listen to the whole recording and write the correct letter in the boxes.

1 The man's ticket costs

A 76€
B 6,70€
C 67€

2 The woman wants to buy a ticket for

A today
B tomorrow
C next week

3 The train arrives in Madrid at

A 14.45
B 15.30
C 13.30

News headlines

Look at the news headlines on a Spanish internet site from time to time. You may be surprised at what you can understand!

Los titulares

la discriminación	discrimination
el prejuicio	prejudice
la lotería	the lottery
el robo	robbery
el ataque cardíaco	heart attack
la marea negra	oil spill
la selva	forest
la sequía	drought
la inundación	flood
la tarjeta de crédito	credit card
el extranjero	foreigner
amenazar	to threaten
detenerse	to be arrested

Word families

Learning groups of words together and making mind maps is a great way of learning more vocabulary and preparing yourself for more difficult texts. When you learn a new noun, verb or adjective see if there are any other related words.

> seco   dry ➡ sequía drought

> consumir   to consume ➡
> el consumidor   the consumer ➡
> el consumo   consumption

> robar to steal ➡ el robo robbery

Worked example

Read the headlines.

> **Los trenes se retrasan a causa de fuerte inundación en Andalucía**

> Detenidos dos extranjeros en Madrid por presunto tráfico de drogas

> **Siria afronta hoy el riesgo de una guerra civil**

> Hacker francés roba más de 40 mil números de tarjetas de crédito

> **Sequía causa estragos con severos incendios forestales en China**

What happened in Madrid?

Two foreigners have been arrested for drug trafficking.

Unfamiliar words

- In texts such as these, there may be words you have never seen before. Revise vocabulary carefully to give yourself the best preparation. Then use strategies to work out unfamiliar words.
- Sometimes Spanish words add an -o or an -a to the end of a word ending in a consonant in English.
- Use related words in Spanish to help you. If you know el retraso (delay), you can work out retrasarse (to be delayed).

> el riesgo is a near cognate – i.e. it sounds similar to the English word 'risk'.

Now try this

Read the news headlines again and answer these questions.

1 Where are forest fires happening?
2 What crime took place online? Mention **two** things.

The environment

To aim for a top grade in speaking or writing, try to include reference to complex issues such as the environment.

El medio ambiente

Los problemas más graves son ...
The most serious problems are ...

la destrucción de la capa del ozono
the destruction of the ozone layer

el efecto invernadero
the greenhouse effect

el uso de los productos químicos
use of chemical products

los animales en peligro de extinción
animals in danger of extinction

la contaminación del aire   air pollution

el calentamiento global   global warming

la guerra   war

la pobreza   poverty

la deforestación   deforestation

el aumento del tráfico   increasing traffic

los gases de escape   exhaust fumes

la lluvia ácida   acid rain

Phrases with the subjunctive

Grammar
page 101

Learn some expressions that use the subjunctive to improve your speaking and show you can use complex structures.

Use the present subjunctive after these expressions:

Es importante que ...   It's important that ...

Es esencial que ...   It's essential that ...

Es increíble que ...   It's incredible that ...

Es terrible que ...   It's terrible that ...

Es importante que separemos la basura.
It's important that we sort our rubbish.

Worked example

¿Cuáles son los problemas del planeta más graves?

> Para mí, el problema más grande es el calentamiento global. Pienso que debemos usar más el transporte público y reutilizar más productos.

AIMING HIGHER

> Es esencial que trabajemos contra la destrucción de la capa del ozono si queremos salvar nuestro planeta. Es necesario que reciclemos más y no deberíamos malgastar la electricidad ni consumir tanta energía. Además, compraré pilas recargables y nunca más utilizaré las bolsas plásticas.

Speaking strategies

Try not to use English sounds when you hesitate, such as 'um' or 'er'. Instead, fill any gaps with Spanish equivalents – pues, a ver, es decir.

This is a satisfactory answer but it could be improved.

Here various tenses are used effectively, as well as the subjunctive: **Es esencial que trabajemos ... / Es necesario que reciclemos ...** The use of connectives and conjunctions such as **si** and **además** also help raise the level.

Now try this

Now prepare your own answers for a speaking assessment. Aim to talk for one minute.
- What are the most serious problems facing the planet today? What is causing them?
- What can people to do improve the situation?

Had a look ☐   Nearly there ☐   Nailed it! ☐

Environmental issues

Make sure you learn a broad range of environment vocabulary.

¡Cuida tu entorno local!

los problemas medioambientales environmental problems	
la basura	rubbish
el reciclaje	recycling
los residuos orgánicos	compostable waste
el cartón	cardboard
el contenedor	container
el atasco	traffic jam
Es importante ...	It's important ...
separar la basura...	to sort / recycle your rubbish
tirar	to throw (away)
usar el transporte público	to use public transport
proteger la naturaleza	to protect nature
apagar las luces	to turn off lights
reciclar el vidrio	to recycle glass

The perfect tense

Grammar page 99

At Foundation level, you need to know the most common verbs in the perfect tense:

He usado el transporte público en Londres
I have used public transport in London

At Higher level, you need to know how to use the perfect tense of a wider range of verbs, including irregular verbs

He puesto el vidrio en el contenedor de reciclaje.
I have put the glass in the recycling container.

Ahorro energía / electricidad.
I save electricity.

Worked example

target A-A*

What has each person been trying to save to help the environment?

Write the correct letter in the box. C

A	Glass	D	Paper
B	Water	E	Clothes
C	Electricity	F	Batteries

En casa he puesto avisos en las paredes de las habitaciones para que mi familia recuerde apagar las luces después de usarlas.

EXAM ALERT!

Here are a few tips for this type of question:

- Always read the categories carefully first to help you look for clues when you read the texts.
- Students often struggle with the vocabulary in this section, so make sure you learn the key words relating to environmental issues.
- Try to work out new words from what the rest of the sentence means.

Students have struggled with exam questions similar to this – **be prepared!**

Now try this

target A-A*

Read the texts and write the correct letter in the boxes.

1 Mi hermano ha dejado contenedores en el jardín para ayudarnos a separar la basura. Incluso tenemos un contenedor para todo lo que nos queda pequeño y que ya no queremos ponernos. ☐

2 La sequía es un gran problema para mucha gente en el mundo. Por eso todos tenemos la responsabilidad de cerrar el grifo mientras nos lavamos los dientes. ☐

What I do to be 'green'

Make sure you learn how to use 'if' clauses to show off in your writing assessment.

Como ser 'verde'

evitar	to avoid
reducir	to reduce
correr el riesgo de	to run the risk of
aumentar	to increase
reducir	to reduce
malgastar	to waste
dedicarse a	to devote time to / to try to
lograr	to achieve
ocuparse de	to be concerned with
ponerse a	to start
quejarse de	to complain about
en vez de	instead of
el desperdicio de agua	wasting water
el bonobús	bus pass
las bolsas plásticas	plastic bags
el alquiler de coches	renting cars
los CFCs	CFC (aerosol) gases
los combustibles fósiles	fossil fuels
los productos ecológicos	green products

'If' clauses

In clauses with si (if), you need to use the correct verb forms:

- Si + present tense + future tense

Si no malgastamos la energía, será mejor para el medio ambiente.

If we don't waste electricity, it will be better for the environment.

- Si + imperfect subjunctive + conditional

Si todo el mundo se dedicara a no utilizar las bolsas plásticas, no habría tanto residuo tóxico.

If everyone tried not to use plastic bags, there would not be as much toxic waste.

Worked example WRITING

What do you do to be 'green'?

Quiero proteger el planeta y por eso siempre separo la basura. Reciclo el vidrio, el papel y el plástico y siempre uso los contenedores correctos.

AIMING HIGHER

Sin duda me ocupo mucho del medio ambiente. Mi familia siempre compra productos ecológicos ya que no contienen productos químicos malos. He comprado el bonobús así que puedo usar el transporte público a menudo y es barato. Claro que es mejor que viajar en coche todo el tiempo. Si más gente se pusiera a andar o ir en autobús, reduciríamos la contaminación del aire.

This piece of writing will achieve a higher level as there is a good range of verb forms:

- **compra, contienen** ➡ present
- **he comprado** ➡ perfect
- **se pusiera** ➡ imperfect subjunctive
- **reduciríamos** ➡ conditional

It also contains some interesting conjunctions **ya que** and **así que** as well as connectives such as **claro que** and **sin duda**.

Now try this WRITING

Write a text answering the following bullet points. Aim to write 100 words.

- What do you do at home at the moment to help the environment?
- What sorts of things have you and your family done recently?
- What do you plan to do in the future?

School subjects

You need to be able to say what subjects you study, and what you think of them and why.

Las asignaturas

Estudio ... I study ...

el arte dramático | el francés | la geografía | la música

la tecnología | el inglés | la educación física | la historia

la informática | el dibujo | las matemáticas | las ciencias

Giving opinions

- **me gusta** (I like) literally translates as 'it pleases me'.
- If the subject is plural, use **me gustan**.
- **me encanta** (I love) and **me interesa** (I'm interested in) behave in the same way.

Me gusta la química.	I like chemistry.
Me encanta el español.	I love Spanish.
Me interesan las ciencias.	I'm interested in science.

Other ways to give your opinion:

Odio / Detesto	I hate
Encuentro	I find
Creo / Pienso	I think
Es / Son ...	It's / They're ...

interesante / fácil / útil / divertido / práctico
interesting / easy / useful / practical

difíciles / aburridos / inútiles / complicados
difficult / boring / useless / complicated

Worked example LISTENING 47 target D

What does Marcela say about school?
Write the correct letter in the box.

A She enjoys studying languages.

B English is more useful than French.

C She did exams in January.

☐ A

– Buenos días, señor director. Soy Marcela.

– Hola, Marcela, ¿qué te gustaría estudiar en enero?

– Me gustan mucho el inglés y el francés. Es muy útil estudiar idiomas.

EXAM ALERT!

Remember that you need to listen for sense as well as specific vocabulary. In this question, as 'science' is an answer option, you'll be listening for **ciencias** – but it doesn't come up. Candidates who don't make the link between **química** (chemistry) and science get questions like this wrong.

Students have struggled with exam questions similar to this – **be prepared!**

Look out for other **links**: here, the **inglés / francés** link to languages is a useful one to spot.

Now try this LISTENING 48 target D

Listen to the rest of the recording.

1 What subject does Juanita like least?

A IT   **B** French   **C** Drama

☐

2 What does Francisco plan to study next year?

A PE   **B** Technology   **C** Science

☐

School description

You can use this page to talk about the facilities at your school.

Mi colegio

Mi colegio es grande / pequeño / moderno.
My school is big / small / modern.

(No) hay ...	There is(n't) ...
(No) tenemos ...	We (don't) have ...
unos laboratorios	science laboratories
unos vestuarios	changing rooms
unas aulas	classrooms
un gimnasio	a gym
una biblioteca	a library
una sala de profesores	a staffroom
un campo de deportes	sports pitch
una piscina	a swimming pool
un salón de actos	a hall
un patio	a playground
las instalaciones	facilities

buenos / malos profesores
good / bad teachers

algunos alumnos traviesos
a few badly-behaved students

Using the verb tener in different tenses

Tener (to have) is a verb you need to know. Be ready to use it in different tenses. It is a radical changing verb (note the vowel change in the present).

	Present	Preterite	Future
I	tengo	tuve	tendré
you	tienes	tuviste	tendrás
he / she / it	tiene	tuvo	tendrá
we	tenemos	tuvimos	tendremos

Remember: you use tener to talk about age: Tengo dieciséis años. I'm 16.

Tenemos un comedor.
We have a canteen.

Worked example

Describe your school.

Mi instituto es grande y moderno con muy buenas instalaciones, por eso me gusta mucho. No teníamos muchas instalaciones deportivas pero ahora hay una piscina grande y el año que viene van a construir una nueva pista de atletismo.

 As well as using the **present** tense to describe your school, add a **past tense** form of **tener** (**teníamos**) and a **future tense** verb (**van a construir**) to improve your answer.

AIMING HIGHER Por lo general, las instalaciones de mi instituto son antiguas pero aceptables, por eso me parece un instituto bastante bueno. No teníamos muchos campos de deportes así que se construyeron una nueva pista de atletismo. Lo bueno es que habrá nuevas aulas porque van a construir nuevos edificios el año que viene.

This student raised her level by including more detail. Using an impersonal structure like **se construyeron** (they built) also shows that you know and can use a wider range of structures accurately.

Now try this

Describe your school. Write at least 100 words.
- Say what facilities it has and does not have.
- Include details of how it has changed / will change.

School routine

You need to be able to understand and describe your school routine, using appropriate verbs.

La rutina del colegio

Llego a las ocho.
I arrive at eight o'clock.

Las clases empiezan a las ocho y media.
Classes start at eight thirty.

Como algo en el recreo.
I have a snack at break.

Charlo con mis amigos.
I chat to my friends.

Las clases terminan a las tres y media.
Classes finish at three thirty.

Tengo entrenamiento de rugby.
I have rugby training.

Hago mis deberes. I do my homework.

Voy al instituto. I go to school.

en invierno / verano in winter / summer

cuando llueve when it rains

Time

Time crops up in all sorts of contexts. It's vital that you know it really well – so keep reviewing it regularly.

 Es la una.

 Son las nueve.

 Son las diez y cuarto.

 Son las once y media.

 en coche

 en autobús

a pie

 en bicicleta

Worked example

 target C

Read the text and answer the question.

> Por la mañana, en invierno, me llevan al instituto en coche los padres de mi amigo, pero en verano voy a pie porque odio viajar en autobús. Llego a las siete y media y las clases terminan a las cuatro todos los días, menos el miércoles que terminamos a las tres.
>
> Mi prima Paula va andando al instituto pero cuando llueve coge el autobús. Llega a las ocho y media y charla con sus amigos. Las clases terminan a las cuatro. El viernes va a un club de ajedrez. **Manu**

Name two ways Manu travels to school.
<u>By car (his friend's parents') and walks</u>

EXAM ALERT!

When writing answers in English, do not use an oblique (/) and don't give more than the required information as the examiner cannot choose the correct options for you. You need to use commas or other conjunctions to give more than one piece of information.

Students have struggled with exam questions similar to this – **be prepared!**

If you wrote by car / walking / bus, that would have resulted in an incorrect answer, as the text states **odio viajar en autobús** (I hate travelling by bus) which is not a correct option for this question.

Now try this

  target C

Read the text again and complete the activity.

1 At what time does Manu arrive at school and when do classes finish on most days?

2 When does Manu's cousin not walk to school?

3 Where does his cousin go on Friday after school?

Comparing schools

Be prepared to compare Spanish schools with schools in your own country.

Mi colegio, tu colegio

en España ...   in Spain ...

Los alumnos llaman a sus profesores por su nombre.
Students call their teachers by their first name.

No estudian ciertas asignaturas.
They do not study certain subjects.

Las vacaciones son más largas.
The holidays are longer.

Hay menos exámenes.
There are fewer exams.

El día escolar es más corto.
The school day is shorter.

Ellos no comen en el instituto.
They don't eat lunch at school.

el bachillerato
Spanish equivalent A level qualification (baccalaureate)

Los alumnos no tienen que llevar uniforme.

Aiming higher

Avoid using me gusta and odio all the time – stand out from the crowd by using something more impressive ...

No lo aguanto. I can't stand it.	No lo aguantaba. I couldn't stand it.
No lo soporto. I can't bear it.	No lo soportaba. I couldn't bear it.
No me importa. I don't mind.	No me importaba. I didn't mind.
Me inquieta. It worries me.	Me inquietaba. It worried me.
No es justo. It's not fair.	No era justo. It wasn't fair.
Me da igual. I'm not bothered about ...	Me daba igual. I wasn't bothered about ...

Worked example

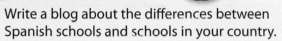

Write a blog about the differences between Spanish schools and schools in your country.

En Inglaterra los alumnos llevan uniforme y no lo soporto, pero visité un instituto español durante un intercambio y ¡qué sorpresa! los alumnos españoles no tenían que llevar uniforme.

AIMING HIGHER
En Inglaterra, los alumnos llevan uniforme pero existen unos pocos institutos privados y públicos dónde no lo llevan. Yo no lo soporto porque es tan incómodo como feo. En abril visité un instituto español y me di cuenta de que los alumnos no llevaban uniforme. ¡Qué envidia!

- Use of **other tenses** (visité) adds sophistication to your language.
- **Exclamation phrases** are also useful to show opinions.

Using more advanced past tense opinions **me di cuenta que** (I realised that) makes your language more complex. The inclusion of a conditional such as **preferiría** (I would prefer) means you would score even more highly.

- Work in a range of **opinions** (and use exclamation phrases where appropriate).
- Express a **preference**.

Now try this

Write about the differences between Spanish schools and schools in your country.
Aim to write at least 100 words.

At primary school

Use the imperfect tense to talk about what you used to do at primary school.

En la escuela primaria

Cuando tenía diez años ... When I was 10 ...

Iba a una escuela de primaria cerca de mi casa.
I used to go to a primary school near my house.

Tenía más / menos amigos.
I used to have more / fewer friends.

Jugaba al fútbol en el patio durante los recreos.
I used to play football in the playground at break.

No estudiaba español.
I didn't study Spanish.

Leíamos cada día.
We used to read every day.

Usaba muchos lápices de colores.
I used to use lots of colouring pencils.

Hacía más deporte.
I used to do more sport.

Comía bocadillos todos los días.
I used to eat sandwiches every day.

Imperfect tense

Grammar page 96

The imperfect tense is used to describe what USED TO HAPPEN or what WAS HAPPENING.

It is formed as follows:

hablar to speak	comer to eat	vivir to live
hablaba	comía	vivía
hablabas	comías	vivías
hablaba	comía	vivía
hablábamos	comíamos	vivíamos
hablabais	comíais	vivíais
hablaban	comían	vivían

Exam strategies

Learn tenses by chanting them – hablaba, hablabas, hablaba ... Start off by reading them, then close your book and see how many you can chant without looking. Keep going until you can do the whole verb.

Worked example

WRITING

Describe your life at primary school.

AIMING HIGHER
En la escuela primaria, cuando tenía apenas nueve años, era bastante perezosa y la escuela me parecía aburrida. Estudiaba menos asignaturas porque no nos enseñaban ni química ni física. Antes, la lengua que más me gustaba era el francés pero ahora prefiero el alemán. De pequeña la vida era más fácil, no tenía tantos deberes y los profesores eran menos severos.

CONTROLLED ASSESSMENT

Present your work neatly and carefully. Each year, illegible handwriting means examiners cannot award higher levels, as they cannot read the Spanish used!

Aiming higher

✓ Including imperfect verbs shows a confident and secure use of a past tense.

✓ Opinions in a range of tenses (me gustaba, prefiero) also show off your range of language.

Now try this

WRITING

• Re-read your work to check for accuracy.
• Check any words you are unsure of in a dictionary.

Describe your life at primary school. Write at least 100 words.

Rules at school

This page gives you the language to talk about school rules and what you think of them.

Las reglas del colegio

No se puede ser desobediente ni maleducado.
You can't be badly behaved or rude.
No se debe hablar mientras que habla el professor.
You should not talk while the teacher is talking.
Se debe pedir permiso.
You have to ask permission.
Las reglas son tontas / necesarias / útiles / inútiles / antecuadas.
The rules are stupid / necessary / useful / useless / out of date.

(No) se puede ...	You can (can't) ...
No se debe ...	You shouldn't ...
llevar maquillaje	wear make-up
comer chicle	chew gum
usar el móvil en clase	use your mobile in class
mandar mensajes	send messages
llegar tarde	arrive late

Key verbs + the infinitive

	querer to want	poder to be able	deber to ought
I	quiero	puedo	debo
you	quieres	puedes	debes
he / she / it	quiere	puede	debe
we	queremos	podemos	debemos
you	queréis	podéis	debéis
they	quieren	pueden	deben

Quiere llevar pendientes pero no se puede llevar joyas.
She wants to wear earrings but you can't wear jewellery.

Worked example

¿Existen normas en tu instituto?

En mi instituto no se puede comer chicle pero la comida del comedor es terrible y me gusta comer chicle después de comer. En mi opinión, las normas son inútiles y tontas pero algunas personas piensan que son necesarias.

Use a variety of **opinion** words and **adjectives** (inútiles, terrible, tontas) to say not only what you think, but also what others think – this will allow you to show off more of what you know.

 AIMING HIGHER En mi instituto la mayoría de las reglas son inútiles. Acaban de introducir una nueva: no se permite usar el móvil en clase. ¡Qué horror! Creo que muchas normas en los colegios son tontas y anticuadas. Todos los profesores piensan que son necesarias y algunos alumnos están de acuerdo.

- Use **idiomatic phrases** such as **acaban de** (they have just).
- Try adding an exclamation phrase as well (**¡Qué horror!**).
- Aim to use more original adjectives. Here this student uses **anticuadas** (old-fashioned) and **necesarias**.

Now try this

¿Existen reglas en tu instituto?
Talk for at least one and a half minutes and try to include:

- 3 opinions / adjectives
- 3 connectives
- 3 different phrases with the infinitive
- a Spanish exclamation

Problems at school

Use this page to talk about the pressures and problems teenagers face at school.

Los problemas en el cole

Se debería ...	You should ...
No se debería ...	You shouldn't ...
sacar buenas notas	get good marks
sacar malas notas	get bad marks
repasar los apuntes	revise
aprobar	pass
intimidar	intimidate
fracasar	fail
echar la culpa	blame
pelearse	fight
respetar	respect
insultar	insult
molestar	annoy

el acoso escolar	bullying	estresante	stressful
una pelea	a fight	débil	weak
los exámenes	exams	torpe	clumsy
las pruebas	tests	insolente	rude

The personal 'a'

When the direct object of a verb is a person, you add a before the person. This is not translated into English.

Miguel intimida a otros alumnos.

Miguel intimidates other pupils.

No se debería insultar a los demás.

You should not insult other people.

Worked example LISTENING 49 target B-C

What problem at school is mentioned? Write the correct letter in the box.

A Bullying
B Messy environment
C No free time
D Pressure to do well
E Timetable clashes
F Journey to school

☐ D

Yo tengo miedo de no aprobar los exámenes. Mis padres esperan mucho de mí.

EXAM ALERT!

This layout and style of question is common. Avoid common errors such as just listening for one or two specific words. Think about all possible words that may be applicable for each category. So for bullying, don't just focus on **acoso** but listen for **intimidar** (to intimidate), **insultar** (to insult), **molestar** (to annoy), **pelearse** (to fight), **una pelea** (a fight) etc.

Students have struggled with exam questions similar to this – **be prepared!**

Now try this LISTENING 50 target B-C

Listen to the rest of the recording and complete the activity.

1 ☐   2 ☐

Future education plans

Use ir with the infinitive to talk about what you're going to do when you finish school.

Qué hacer en el futuro

el año que viene / el año próximo	next year
en el futuro	in the future
No estoy seguro/a ...	I'm not sure ...
Si saco buenas notas ...	If I get good grades ...
Voy a ...	I'm going to ....
estudiar lenguas / idiomas	study languages
ir a la universidad	go to university
buscar / encontrar un empleo	look for / find a job
tomar un año libre / sabático	take a gap year
tener éxito	be successful

seguir estudiando en mi instituto
continue studying in my school

ir a otro instituto para alumnos de 16 a 18 años
go to a sixth-form college

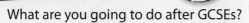

ganar mucho dinero
earn lots of money

Near future tense

Grammar page 97

This form of the future, (using ir + infinitive) is like the English 'going to', and is used to express plans and intentions.

I	voy		ir
you	vas		buscar
he / she / it	va	a	hacer
we	vamos		seguir
you	vais		trabajar
they	van		estudiar

Voy a ir a la universidad.
I'm going to go to university.

Va a estudiar música.
He is going to study music.

Worked example

WRITING

What are you going to do after GCSEs?

El año que viene voy a estudiar idiomas porque me encanta el español y es fácil e interesante.

AIMING HIGHER

Quiero seguir estudiando el año próximo. Me gustaría estudiar idiomas porque me encanta saber más de otras culturas. Es más, saqué buenas notas el año pasado en español. Si sigo sacando buenas notas en el futuro, iré a la universidad porque quiero ser traductora en la Unión Europea.

Aiming higher

✓ VARY your tenses – this makes your answer more interesting and lets you show off what you know.

✓ DEVELOP your answer – always look for opportunities to add more information, e.g. Es más, saqué buenas notas el año pasado ...

✓ Make it STAND OUT – an unusual twist will help distinguish it, e.g. quiero ser traductora en la Unión Europea. (I want to be a translator in the European Union.)

✓ IMPRESS with interesting structures: Si sigo sacando buenas notas en el futuro, iré ... (If I keep getting good grades in the future, I will go ...).

Now try this

WRITING

What are you going to do after GCSEs? Write at least 50 words.

Check your own writing against the AQA GCSE marking criteria. How well have you done? How can you improve?

Future plans

Using the future tense and the subjunctive will help improve your mark.

Tus planes para el futuro

cuando sea mayor ...	when I'm older ...
cuando termine la universidad ...	when I finish university ...
Trabajaré como ...	I'll work as ...
Trabajaré en el extranjero.	I'll work abroad.
Voy a casarme y tener hijos.	I'm going to get married and have children.
Seré rico.	I'll be rich.
Ganaré la lotería.	I'll win the lottery.
Seré muy feliz.	I will be very happy.
Viajaré mucho.	I'll travel a lot.
Ganaré mucho dinero.	I'll earn lots of money.

Es un campo en el que me gustaría trabajar.
It's a field in which I would like to work.

Seré famoso.
I'll be famous.

Subjunctive

Grammar page 101

The subjunctive is used after **cuando** to talk about an event in the future.

Cuando tenga veinte años, viajaré mucho.
When I'm 20, I'll travel a lot.

To form the subjunctive, add the following endings to the infinitive:

hablar to speak	comer to eat	vivir to live
hable	coma	viva
hables	comas	vivas
hable	coma	viva
hablemos	comamos	vivamos
habléis	comáis	viváis
hablen	coman	vivan

Worked example SPEAKING

¿Cuáles son tus planes para el futuro?

En el futuro viajaré mucho y ganaré mucho dinero, así que seré feliz porque podré comprar mucha ropa.

AIMING HIGHER Cuando sea mayor y termine la universidad viajaré por el mundo. Ganaré mucho dinero trabajando como comerciante así que seré feliz porque podré comprar muchas cosas nuevas. Tengo la intención de probar suerte en los Estados Unidos.

Use the future tense (**viajaré, ganaré**) to say what you will do.

Use connectives (**así que, porque**) to justify your opinions and give a more detailed response.

This answer uses a greater variety of structures. The **gerund** is used as a linking word for two clauses: **ganaré mucho dinero trabajando como comerciante** (I will earn a lot of money working in business).

The subjunctive is used to add variety: **cuando sea mayor y cuando termine la universidad ...** (when I am older and when I finish university ...)

Now try this SPEAKING

¿Cuáles son tus planes para el futuro?
Talk for at least one minute.

Try to include:
- one or two subjunctive phrases
- two or three future tense phrases.

Jobs

Use this page to talk about the different jobs people do.

Empleos

abogado	azafata	bombero	camarero
lawyer	air hostess	fireman	waiter

enfermero	médico	obrero	veterinario
nurse	doctor	worker	vet

actor / actriz	actor
ama de casa	housewife
cartero/a	postman / postwoman
cajero/a	cashier
cocinero/a	cook / chef
dentista	dentist
escritor / escritora	writer
panadero/a	baker
peluquero/a	hairdresser
periodista	journalist
policía	policeman / policewoman
secretario/a	secretary
estar en paro	to be unemployed

Using ser to say what jobs people do

Use the verb ser to say what jobs people do. Note that you omit the definite article (un / una).

Soy cocinero.   I'm a cook.

Es modelo.   She's a model.

Es camarero.
He's a waiter.

Feminine forms

If the job is done by a woman, change -o to -a:

cocinero – cocinera   camarero – camarera

> Note some exceptions:
> actor   actriz
> Same in masculine / feminine:
> médico, dentista, policía

trabajar in different tenses

Present	Imperfect	Future
trabajo	trabajaba	trabajaré
I work	I used to work	I will work

Worked example

 LISTENING 51   target B-C

Listen and answer question 1.

1 How old is Paco? `30`
2 Which job did he use to do?
3 Why did he stop doing that job?
4 What does he do now?
5 What job will he do in the future?
6 Why does he want to do this job?

– Hola. Me llamo Paco y tengo treinta años.

Listening strategies

- If the questions are in English, you must ANSWER IN ENGLISH
- You'll hear every recording TWICE so don't worry if you don't catch all the answers on first listening.
- If you've missed an answer, go on to the next question.
- Don't simply write down the first relevant word you hear. Make sure you listen to the END of a recording before you make your final decision.

Now try this

 LISTENING 52   target B-C

Listen to the whole recording and complete the rest of the activity.

Job adverts

Job adverts could come up in your reading exam, so learn the words on this page.

Ofertas de empleo

rellenar una ficha	to fill in a form
un anuncio	an advert
una solicitud	an application
el título	university degree
el horario de trabajo	hours of work
las condiciones de trabajo	working conditions
una entrevista	an interview
estar encargado de	to be in charge of
el jefe / la jefa	the boss
un empleo / un trabajo	a job
una carta	a letter
por hora	per hour
una respuesta	an answer
solicitar un empleo	to apply for a job
a tiempo parcial / completo	part / full time
en una empresa	in a company
con un buen sueldo	with a good salary

Prepositions

Prepositions come up in every topic: they give information about WHERE, WHEN and HOW things happen.

a	to / at	entre	between
con	with	para	for / in order to
de	from / of		
desde	from, since	por	for / by
en	in, on	sin	without
		sobre	on, about

en nuestra página web	on our web page
por fax	by fax
para tener más información	in order to have more information
sin experiencia	without experience

Worked example  **target C**

Read the text.

> **OFERTAS DE EMPLEO**
> Multimundo – Se necesita secretario sin experiencia para trabajar a tiempo parcial en una empresa multinacional. Interesados sólo deben rellenar una ficha en nuestra página web. Ofrecemos un buen sueldo y un horario de trabajo flexible. Las entrevistas tendrán lugar en un mes.

Write the letter of **one** correct statement in the box.

A The company has branches in different countries.
B You should look at the web page for more information.
C Training isn't mentioned.
D The salary is good.
E The hours of work are long.
F The interviews will take place in a month.

A

Reading strategies

- Size does matter! Make sure you learn non topic specific small but very important words. Make a list of them and learn them carefully. Words such as: sin (without), nunca (never), siempre (always), sólo (only).

- It's a good idea to underline or highlight the key words in the questions or statements on your exam paper to help you focus your attention and look for the relevant information in the text.

- Read carefully to pick up the detail as well as the gist.

 Now try this **target C**

Read the text again and complete the two boxes with the letters for the remaining **two** correct statements.

☐ ☐

CV

You may encounter a CV in a reading exam or writing assessment. If you are creating one, remember to avoid lists and very short sentences.

CV

Nombre y apellido
Paul Jones

Dirección
3 Blake Road, Anytown
AT1 2AZ, Inglaterra

Estado civil   casado

Fecha de nacimiento   13/12/88

Experiencia profesional   camarero

Cualidades personales   animado

Aficiones   tenis y fútbol

Idiomas   inglés y español

Correo electrónico   pauljones@email.co.uk

Reading strategies

It is easy to work out what the headings in the CV mean by looking at how Paul has filled it in. Using the context to work out the meaning of unknown words is a very useful strategy.

Review **personality adjectives** and the vocabulary for **activities** and **hobbies** in preparation for writing a CV.

Worked example

Read this section from Paul's CV. and write the correct letter in the box.

Cualidades personales: simpático, sensible, trabajador, fiable, comprensivo

Paul is ...
A sympathetic
B friendly
C popular

☐ B

Cognates are helpful but watch out for **false friends**! Words don't always mean what they seem to. Many students find these three adjectives confusing:
simpático – sensible – comprensivo
Can you use the activity to work out their correct meanings?

Logical thinking!

Remember to think LOGICALLY. Is it likely that someone would use negative adjectives to describe him/herself on a CV? The answer may help you rule out some options.

Now try this

Read Paul's whole CV, and complete the activity.

1 Paul is ...
A single
B divorced
C married
☐

2 Paul used to work as a ...
A lorry driver
B waiter
C tennis coach
☐

3 Paul describes his personality as ...
A ambitious
B active
C cheerful
☐

4 He speaks ...
A English
B Spanish and French
C Spanish and English
☐

Had a look ☐   Nearly there ☐   Nailed it! ☐

Job application

Job applications may come up in the reading or listening exam, so learn key phrases.

Solicitud de empleo

I am writing to apply for the post of journalist published on the web

| I attach my curriculum vitae |

| as you can see |

| I am a ... worker |

| I work well |

Muy señor mío:

Me dirijo a usted para solicitar el puesto de periodista publicado en la página web www.empleos.es el día 23 de agosto. En este momento trabajo como escritor para una empresa puntocom.

Le adjunto mi currículum vitae y como podrá ver tengo mucha experiencia.

Soy un trabajador eficiente, rápido y siempre trabajo bien en equipo. Soy bilingüe en español e inglés y domino perfectamente el francés. Hablo un poco de alemán. Manejo bien la informática.

Quedo a su disposición.

Le saluda atentamente

Pablo García

| I am bilingual in ... |

| I am a competent user of French. |

| I await your reply. |

Worked example

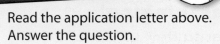

Read the application letter above. Answer the question.

Name **two** of his strengths that don't relate to his linguistic ability.

He is an efficient worker / He works well in a team

Make sure you are familiar with the AQA vocabulary list so that words like **periodista** (journalist) don't catch you out.

Now try this

1 What job is advertised and what must the job seeker have?
2 When are you expected to work?
3 Where exactly will the interviews take place?

Se buscan dependientes con experiencia en vender directamente al cliente. El horario de trabajo es fijo y hay que trabajar todos los días, domingos incluidos. Sin embargo, las tiendas están cerradas los lunes. Interesados deben mandar una carta y el curriculum vitae por fax. Las entrevistas tendrán lugar en nuestras tiendas de ropa del centro de la ciudad.

Job interview

As well as the job interview vocabulary here, review personality adjectives to prepare fully for this topic.

Una entrevista de empleo

¿Por qué quiere ser … ?
Why do you want to be … ?

Quiero ser … porque me fascina.
I want to be a … because it fascinates me.

Me encantaría trabajar con …
I would love to work with …

¿Qué experiencia tiene?
What experience do you have?

He trabajado como / para …
I have worked as / for …

Tengo experiencia laboral en …
I have experience working in …

He trabajado en equipo / solo antes.
I have worked in a team / alone before.

¿Qué cualidades tiene?
What qualities do you have?

Soy entusiasta / competente / ambicioso.
I am enthusiastic / competent / ambitious.

¿Puede decirme algo más sobre …?
Can you tell me more about …?

He escrito …   I have written …

He creado …   I have created …

Perfect tense

Grammar page 99

The perfect tense describes what someone HAS DONE or something that HAS HAPPENED.

- To form the perfect tense, use:
  haber in the present tense + past participle.
- To form the past participle:
  take off ar / er / ir from the infinitive and add ado / ido / ido.

I	he	
you	has	
he / she / it	ha	hablado
we	hemos	bebido
you	habéis	venido
they	han	

He trabajado en un hotel antes.
I have worked in a hotel before.

Worked example

 53   target A

Listen and answer the question.
What does Ramona want to do and why?

She wants to be an air hostess as she loves to work with people.

Cuando era más joven pensaba ser dentista. Ahora, más que nada, quiero ser azafata porque me encanta trabajar con gente.

Exam strategies

- Don't be put off by what you DON'T understand. Remember that you don't have to understand every word.
- Read the questions before you listen so that you know the type of language / information you are listening out for.
- You will have **five** minutes to do this. Don't be distracted by irrelevant detail.

Now try this

 54   target A

Listen to the rest of the recording and complete the activity.

1 What did Ramona do previously and why exactly did she stop?
2 Why doesn't she want to work for Iberia again?
3 What is the negative side of the job mentioned?
4 What two personal characteristics does Ramona mention about herself?

Listen carefully for **opinions** – and wait until they are fully expressed. Don't jump to conclusions.

Opinions about jobs

Be ready to understand and give a range of opinions on jobs – both positive and negative.

Opiniones sobre empleos 😊

Me gusta la variedad.	I like variety.
Me gusta la flexibilidad.	I like flexibility.
Está bien pagado.	It's well paid.
Me gusta tener responsabilidades.	
I like having responsibility.	
Me encanta trabajar en contacto con la gente.	
I love having contact with people.	
Me encanta trabajar en equipo.	
I love working in a team.	
La ambición es importante	
Ambition is important.	
Hay que tener calificaciones.	
You have to have qualifications.	

Opiniones sobre empleos 🙁

Es un trabajo difícil.	It's a difficult job.
Odio trabajar solo.	I hate working alone.
Está mal pagado.	It's badly paid.
Odio al jefe.	I hate the boss.
Las horas son largas.	The hours are long.
Estoy de pie todo el día.	I'm on my feet all day.
Están en huelga.	They are on strike.
Puede ser estresante.	It can be stressful.
No me gustan los clientes maleducados.	
I don't like rude customers.	

Me gusta ayudar a la gente.
I like helping people.

Es aburrido y monótono.
It's boring and repetitive.

Worked example   READING   target B

Read the texts.

Jorge: El trabajo es importante porque nos enseña a trabajar en equipo y a reconocer el valor del dinero. Se aprende a llevarse bien con otros y a no malgastar lo que ganamos.

Nuria: Antes de tener un sueldo, sólo llevaba ropa de diseño porque mis padres la compraban. Ahora gasto lo menos posible y no me importa tanto estar a la moda. Soy más responsable.

Ramón: A mi modo de ver, las chicas siempre son más trabajadores que los chicos. Casi todas mis amigas trabajan pero tengo varios amigos que están en paro. Las calificaciones son importantes pero las cualidades tienen gran importancia.

Whose shopping habits have changed since starting working? Nuria

EXAM ALERT!

This question type has proved a challenge for candidates in previous papers. The key is focusing on understanding the whole message of the text and not looking for specific ítems of vocabulary.

Students have struggled with exam questions similar to this – **be prepared!**

Linking buying clothes with shopping habits is key here. It is also vital to spot **Antes** followed by **Ahora** ... , which are used to indicate two contrasting facts and point to the fact that a **change** has taken place.

Now try this   READING   target B

Read the text again and complete the activity.

1 Who thinks social skills improve through working?
2 Who mentions boys not finding jobs?
3 Who thinks your grades at school matter less than your attitude when finding work?

Part-time jobs

When talking about a part-time job, use tener que to discuss your responsibilities.

Empleos a tiempo parcial

Reparto periódicos.
I deliver newspapers.

Trabajo como dependiente.
I work as a shop assistant

Corto el césped.
I mow the lawn.

Trabajo como jardinero.
I work as a gardener.

Gano mucho / poco.
I earn a lot / a little.

Cuido a niños.
I look after children.

Es fácil / difícil / interesante / aburrido / variado.
It is easy / difficult / interesting / boring / varied.

los sábados	on Saturdays
después del colegio	after school
Me interesa.	It interests me.
Lo odio.	I hate it.
todos los días	every day

Talking about obligations

To say what you HAVE to do, use tener + que + infinitive:

Tengo que ir bien vestido.
I have to be well dressed.

Tiene que pasear al perro.
She has to walk the dog.

Useful forms of tener:

Tuve que lavar coches.
I had to wash cars.

Tenía que servir comida.
I had to serve food.

Worked example

¿Has tenido un trabajo a tiempo parcial?
El año pasado trabajé en un restaurante como camarero. Tuve que servir comida y me gustó porque me interesa trabajar en equipo.

Justifying your opinion (saying why you like your job) creates a subordinate clause me gustó porque me interesa trabajar en equipo (I liked it because I enjoy working as part of a team).

AIMING HIGHER Todos los sábados trabajo como jardinero. Es muy variado y gano mucho. Ayer tuve que levantarme temprano porque trabajaba todo el día. Fue muy interesante porque tuve que cortar el césped y plantar muchas flores.

Using tener que in the preterite, trabajar in the imperfect (was working) and an opinion phrase in the preterite (fue – it was), makes for a much stronger response.

Now try this

You are applying for a summer job at a campsite. Aim to talk for at least one minute and include:
- personal details
- the kind of work you would like at the campsite and why
- your previous part time jobs, opinions about the work and your reasons.

My work experience

Work experience is a good topic for showing off your knowledge of the imperfect tense.

Experiencia laboral

¿Qué experiencia laboral tienes?
What work experience have you had?

Trabajaba en … | I was working in …
una oficina / una tienda / un instituto | an office / shop / school

Hacía fotocopias. | I made photocopies.

Trabajaba con niños. | I worked with children.

Ayudaba al jefe. | I helped the boss.

Utilizaba el ordenador. | I used the computer.

Ayudaba a los enfermos. | I helped sick people.

Tenía que dar información a los clientes.
I had to give information to customers.

Contestaba al teléfono.
I answered the phone.

Vendía cosas a los clientes.
I sold things to customers.

Imperfect tense: irregular verbs

Grammar page 96

Use the imperfect tense to talk about things you used to do in the past. Only THREE verbs are irregular in the imperfect.

	ir to go	ser to be	ver to see
I	iba	era	veía
you	ibas	eras	veías
he/she/it	iba	era	veía
we	íbamos	éramos	veíamos
you	ibais	erais	veíais
they	iban	eran	veían

Era mi jefe.
He was my boss.

Iba al trabajo en coche.
I used to go to work by car.

Worked example

LISTENING 55 target B-C

Listen. What did Cristina think of her work experience?
Write **P** (positive), **N** (negative) or **P + N** (positive and negative).
Cristina ☐ P

Tengo experiencia laboral como dependienta, ya que trabajaba en una tienda. Para llegar allí, primero tenía que coger el metro y después iba a pie. Era fácil. También tenía que llevar un uniforme cómodo y bonito.

Exam strategies

- Don't rely on opinion phrases (me gustaba / odiaba, etc) to answer this task type. Sometimes there won't be any! Listen out for adjectives too.
- For this type of question, remember that there will always be at least one of each response. So with three extracts, one will be P, one will be N and one will be P + N.

She says that it was easy to get to work (era fácil) and gives a positive description of her uniform using the adjectives **cómodo** (comfortable) and **bonito** (pretty).

Now try this

LISTENING 56 target B-C

Listen to the rest of the recording and complete the activity. Write **P**, **N** or **P+N**.

1 Santi ☐   2 Paula ☐

Work experience

As well as the imperfect, you'll need to know the preterite to talk about work experience.

Experiencia laboral

Era fascinante / duro.
It was exciting / tough.

Me ayudaron mucho.
They helped me a lot.

Estaba encargado/a de …
I was in charge of …

Aprendí mucho.
I learned a lot.

Me trataron bien.
They treated me well.

Terminaba muy cansado.
I was very tired at the end of the day.

Eran muchas horas.
The hours were long.

Los clientes eran antipáticos.
The clients were unpleasant.

Siempre había quejas.
There were always complaints.

No me gustaría trabajar allí.
I wouldn't like to work there.

Imperfect or preterite?

You use the PRETERITE tense for a SINGLE event that took place in the past. You use the IMPERFECT tense for repeated or CONTINUOUS actions in the past. In English we often translate them in the same way.

Archivaba los documentos.
I filed documents. / I used to file documents.

No recibí el sueldo de enero.
I didn't receive January's salary.

El gerente no me trató bien.
The manager did not treat me well.

Worked example SPEAKING

¿Dónde hiciste tu experiencia laboral?

Trabajaba en una agencia de viajes. Eran muchas horas, pero aprendí mucho sobre países diferentes. Me gustó la experiencia.

AIMING HIGHER

Mi experiencia laboral era fascinante. Trabajaba en una residencia de ancianos en un pueblo pequeño. Tenía que trabajar cada noche y por lo tanto terminaba muy cansado pero recibía un buen sueldo y mi jefe me ayudó mucho. Ojalá pudiera seguir trabajando allí durante las vacaciones, pero preferiría no trabajar por la noche.

Aim to use at least two tenses. Here the **imperfect** las horas eran largas (the hours were long) and **preterite** me gustó la experiencia (I liked the experience) are used.

Using a more complex structure (with the **imperfect subjunctive**) and a conditional will really help when aiming for the highest grades: ojalá pudiera seguir trabajando allí durante las vacaciones, pero prefería no trabajar por la noche (he hopes he can continue working there but he would prefer not to work at night).

Now try this SPEAKING

¿Qué experiencia laboral tienes?
Talk about work experience you have done.
Aim to talk for at least one minute.

Aim to include:
• where you were working
• whether you liked it and why (not)
• whether you would like to work there in the future and why (not).

Dialogues and messages

Learn this language to understand, take and leave phone messages.

Diálogos y mensajes

¿Diga / Dígame?
Hello? (when answering the phone)

Si es urgente se puede llamar ...
If it's urgent you can call ...

el teletrabajo	telesales
la llamada	telephone call
Llámame / llámeme.	Call me (informal / formal).
Le llamaré.	I'll call you back.
Te / Le contactaré	I will contact you (informal / formal).
Espere.	Wait.
Le paso.	I will put you through.
en la línea	on the line
de momento	at the moment
por telefóno	by phone
número equivocado	wrong number
después de la señal	after the tone
mi número de móvil	my mobile number

Formal v. informal language

In the workplace, the formal (polite) 'you' – singular usted and plural ustedes – will be used in most situations. Remember that this takes the 3rd PERSON of the verb.

Usted form (formal / polite):
¿Puede llamar más tarde?
Can you call later?

(Ustedes) pueden mandar un email.
You can (all) send an email.

Tú form (familiar):
Puedes dejar un mensaje.
You can leave a message.

Envíame un mensaje de texto.
Send me a text.

Worked example LISTENING 57 target C

Listen to Jesús's answer machine message. Write the correct letter in the box.

According to the recording, Jesús cannot answer the phone because he is ...

A busy **B** out shopping **C** on holiday

C

¡Hola! Ha llamado al contestador automático de Jesús. Ahora no estoy aquí porque me he ido de vacaciones ...

- Remember: you have **five minutes** to look at the questions. Work out the numbers you'll be listening for!

- Spanish **telephone numbers** consist of nine numbers, often starting '9' or '8' for fixed lines and '6' for mobiles. They are normally written as follows: e.g. 657 87 42 19, which would be said: seis, cincuenta y siete; ochenta y siete; cuarenta y dos; diecinueve

---

Now try this LISTENING 58 target C

Listen to the whole recording and complete the activity.

1 Jésus's message states that he will ...

   A return the call tomorrow

   B call back when he returns

   C call your mobile

   ☐

2 His mobile number is ...

   A 677 68 97 78

   B 667 78 96 78

   C 666 78 97 78

   ☐

Nouns and articles

Here you'll find out about the gender of nouns and how to use the correct article.

Gender

Nouns are words that name things and people. Every Spanish noun has a gender – masculine (m) or feminine (f). If a word ends in -o or -a, it's easy to work out the gender.

ends in -o	masculine – el bolso
ends in -a	feminine – la pera

Exceptions:

el día	day	la foto	photo
el turista	tourist	la moto	motorbike
el problema	problem	la mano	hand

For words ending in any other letter, you need to learn the word with the article. If you don't know the gender, look it up in a dictionary.

cine nm cinema

noun　masculine – so **el cine**

The definite article

The definite article ('the') changes to match the gender and number of the noun.

	Singular	Plural
Masculine	el libro	los libros
Feminine	la casa	las casas

The definite article is sometimes used in Spanish when we don't use it in English:

- with abstract nouns (things you can't see/touch)

El turismo es importante.	Tourism is important.

- with likes and dislikes

Me gusta el francés.	I like French.

- with days of the week to say 'on'

el domingo	on Sunday
los domingos	on Sundays

No me gustan nada las ciencias.

I don't like science at all.

The indefinite article

The indefinite article ('a/an') changes to match the gender and number of the noun. In the plural, the English is 'some' or 'any'.

	Singular	Plural
Masculine	un libro	unos libros
Feminine	una casa	unas casas

The indefinite article is NOT used when you talk about jobs.

Soy profesor.　I'm a teacher.

Plurals

Plurals are easy to form in Spanish.

Singular	Plural
ends in a vowel un tomate	add -s unos tomates
ends in any consonant except z la región	add -es las regiones
ends in z el pez	drop z and add -ces los peces

Now try this

1 Make these nouns plural.
   1 folleto ....
   2 vez ....
   3 tradición ....
   4 café ....
   5 actor ....

2 **El** or **la**? Use a dictionary to fill in the articles.
   1 ....ciudad
   2 ....pesticida
   3 ....pintor
   4 ....educación
   5 ....imagen

Adjectives

When using adjectives, you have to think about AGREEMENT and POSITION.

Adjective agreement

Adjectives describe nouns. They must agree with the noun in gender (masculine or feminine) and number (singular or plural).

adjective	Singular	Plural
ending in -o		
masculine	alto	altos
feminine	alta	altas
ending in -e		
masculine	inteligente	inteligentes
feminine	inteligente	inteligentes
ending in a consonant		
masculine	azul	azules
feminine	azul	azules

A dictionary shows the masculine form of an adjective. Make sure you don't forget to make it agree when it's feminine and / or plural!

las faldas amarillas   the yellow skirts

Note the exceptions:

ending in -or		
masculine	hablador	habladores
feminine	habladora	habladoras
adjectives of nationality ending in s		
masculine	inglés	ingleses
feminine	inglesa	inglesas

Position of adjectives

Most Spanish adjectives come AFTER the noun.

una falda azul   a blue skirt

These adjectives always come BEFORE the noun:

mucho	a lot	próximo	next
poco	a little	último	last
primero	first	alguno	some / any
segundo	second	ninguno	none
tercero	third		

Tengo muchos amigos. I have a lot of friends.

grande comes BEFORE the noun when it means 'great' rather than 'big'. It changes to **gran** before both masculine and feminine singular nouns.

Fue una gran película. It was a great film.

Short forms of adjectives

Some adjectives are shortened when they come before a masculine singular noun.

bueno	good	buen
malo	bad	mal
primero	first	primer
alguno	some / any	algún
ninguno	none	ningún

Pablo es un buen amigo. Pablo is a good friend.

Now try this

Complete the text. (Look at the adjective endings to work out where they go.)

bonitas   ruidosos   interesantes   ingleses   pequeña   habladora   históricos   simpática

Mallorca es una isla .... Tiene muchas playas .... En Mallorca hay muchos turistas
.... La gente allí es muy .... y es muy .... Mallorca tiene muchos museos
.... y muchos bares .... Se pueden hacer muchas cosas ....

Possessives and pronouns

Use possessives to talk about who things belong to. Using pronouns will also help you sound more fluent.

Possessive adjectives

Possessive adjectives agree with the noun they describe, NOT the owner, e.g. sus botas – his boots.

	Singular	Plural
my	mi	mis
your	tu	tus
his / her / its	su	sus
our	nuestro/a	nuestros/as
your	vuestro/a	vuestros/as
their	su	sus

mis amigos
my friends

su colegio
their school

Possessive pronouns

These agree with the noun they replace, e.g. Su chaqueta es más elegante que la mía. His jacket is smarter than mine.

	Singular	
mine	el mío	la mía
yours	el tuyo	la tuya
his / hers / its	el suyo	la suya
ours	el nuestro	la nuestra
yours	el vuestro	la vuestra
theirs	el suyo	la suya

	Plural	
mine	los míos	las mías
yours	los tuyos	las tuyas
his / hers / its	los suyos	las suyas
ours	los nuestros	las nuestras
yours	los vuestros	las vuestras
theirs	los suyos	las suyas

Prepositional pronouns

These are used after prepositions.

para – for	mí – me	nosotros/as – us
por – for	ti – you	vosotros/as – you
sin – without	él – him	ellos – them (m)
con – with	ella – her	ellas – them (f)

Esta chaqueta es para ti.
This jacket is for you.

Note the accent on mí.

con + mí ➡ conmigo with me
con + ti ➡ contigo with you

The relative pronoun que

que ('which', 'that' or 'who') allows you to refer back to someone or something already mentioned. You must include it in Spanish, even when you might omit it in English.

El profesor que enseña francés.
The teacher who teaches French.

El libro que lee es español.
The book (that/which) he is reading is Spanish.

Now try this

Circle the correct form each time.

Mis / Mi padrastro se llama Miguel. **Su / Sus** hijas son mis hermanastras. **Mi / Mis** hermanastra, **que / por** se llama Isabel, tiene un novio, Pablo. **Su / Sus** novio es menos guapo que **el mío / la mía**. Salgo con **él / ella** desde hace seis años. Isabel sale con **el suyo / las suyas** desde hace un mes.

Comparisons

If you're aiming for a higher grade, use structures like the comparative and superlative.

The comparative

The comparative is used to compare two things. It is formed as follows:

| más + adjective + que = more … than |
| menos + adjective + que = less … than |
| tan + adjective + como = as … as |

The adjective agrees with the noun it describes.

Madrid es más interesante que Leeds.
Madrid is more interesting than Leeds.

Pablo es menos alto que su hermano.
Pablo is shorter (less tall) than his brother.

Mi habitación es tan pequeña como la tuya.
My bedroom is as small as yours.

The superlative

The superlative is used to compare more than two things. It is formed as follows:

| el/la/los/las (+ noun) + más + adjective = the most … |
| el/la/los/las (+ noun) + menos + adjective = the least … |

The definite article and the adjective agree with the noun described.

El español es el idioma más interesante.
Spanish is the most interesting language.

Esta casa es la menos cara del pueblo.
This house is the least expensive in the village.

Irregulars

Learn these useful irregular forms:

Adjective	Comparative	Superlative
good	better	the best
bueno	mejor	el/la mejor los/las mejores
bad	worse	the worst
malo	peor	el/la peor los/las peores

Este hotel es el mejor de la región.
This hotel is the best in the region.

Los restaurantes de aquí son los peores.
The restaurants here are the worst.

Using -ísimo for emphasis

You can add -ísimo to the end of an adjective to make it stronger.

La chaqueta es carísima.   The jacket is very expensive.

El libro es malísimo.   The book is very bad.

La comida es riquísima.
The food is really delicious.

Don't forget to make adjectives agree!

Now try this

Complete the sentences with the correct comparative or superlative.

1 Este libro es ………… de la serie. (*worst*)
2 Mis hermanos son ………… amigos que tengo. (*best*)
3 La falda es ………… de la tienda. (*prettiest*)
4 Este partido de fútbol es …………. (*really boring*)
5 Carmen es ………… jugadora. (*best*)
6 Este piso es………… que he visto hoy. (*ugliest*)
7 Pablo es…………que Juan. (*better looking*)
8 Mi hermana es …………que mi hermano. (*lazier*)

Other adjectives

Here you can revise demonstrative adjectives and some useful indefinite adjectives.

Demonstrative adjectives

Demonstrative adjectives ('this', 'that', 'these', 'those') agree with their noun in number and gender.

	Masculine	Feminine	
singular	este	esta	this
plural	estos	estas	these
singular	ese	esa	that
plural	esos	esas	those

este móvil	this mobile
esa calculadora	that calculator
esos chicos	those boys
estas chicas	these girls

Using different words for 'that' and 'those'

In Spanish there are two words for 'that' / 'those': ese and aquel. You use aquel to refer to something further away.

esa chica y aquel chico

that girl and that boy (over there)

	Masculine	Feminine	
singular	aquel	aquella	that
plural	aquellos	aquellas	those

Indefinite adjectives

Indefinite adjectives come up in a lot of contexts, so make sure you know how to use them.

cada	each
otro	another
todo	all
mismo	same
algún / alguna	some / any

As with all other adjectives, remember to make them agree.
Exception: **cada** – it doesn't change.

Quisiera otra cerveza.	I would like another beer.
Todos los pasajeros estaban enfadados.	All the passengers were angry.
Llevamos la misma camiseta.	We're wearing the same t-shirt.
¿Tienes algún cuaderno?	Do you have any exercise books?

Cada estudiante tiene su ordenador
Each student has their own computer.

Now try this

Translate into Spanish.

1 That boy is stupid.
2 This apple is tasty.
3 I want to buy those jeans.
4 That house over there is really big.
5 This film is boring.
6 I don't want that jumper – I want that cardigan.

Pronouns

Use pronouns to avoid repeating nouns – it helps make your Spanish more fluent and interesting.

Subject, direct object and indirect object

- The SUBJECT is the person / thing doing the action (shown by the verb).
- The OBJECT is the person / thing having the action (shown by the verb) done to it. It can be DIRECT or INDIRECT.

SUBJECT	VERB	DIRECT OBJECT	INDIRECT OBJECT
Marisa	sends	the e-mail	to David.
She	sends	it	to him.

subject pronoun		direct object pronoun		indirect object pronoun	
I	yo	me	me	(to / for) me	me
you	tú	you	te	(to / for) you	te
he / it	él	him / it	lo	(to / for) him / it	le
she / it	ella	her / it	la	(to / for) her / it	le
we	nosotros/as	us	nos	(to / for) us	nos
you	vosotros/as	you	os	(to / for) you	os
they	ellos / ellas	them	los / las	(to / for) them	les

Subject pronouns aren't often used in Spanish because the verb ending is enough to show who is doing the action. They're sometimes used for EMPHASIS.

A mí me gusta España, pero él quiere ir a Italia.   I like Spain but he wants to go to Italy.

Position of object pronouns

In general, object pronouns come:

- BEFORE the verb

- AFTER a negative

La compré en el supermercado.	I bought it in the supermarket.
No la tengo.	I don't have it.
Nadie les escribe.	No one writes to them.

The object pronoun can be added to the infinitive in the near future tense.

Voy a comprarlo por Internet.   or
Lo voy a comprar por Internet.
I'm going to buy it for my mother.

Object pronouns are attached to the end of an imperative.

¡Hazlo!   Do it!

Now try this

Rewrite the sentences, replacing the words in bold with pronouns.

1 Voy a dar **el regalo** a mi padre.
2 Quiero **a mi hermana**.
3 Voy a comprar **un libro**.
4 Vi **a Katie y Ryan** en Bilbao.
5 Quiero decir **a Pablo** un secreto.

The present tense

This page covers all three types of regular verbs and stem-changing verbs in the present tense.

Present tense (regular)

To form the present tense of regular verbs, replace the infinitive ending as follows:

	hablar – to speak	comer – to eat	vivir – to live
I	hablo	como	vivo
you	hablas	comes	vives
he / she / it	habla	come	vive
we	hablamos	comemos	vivimos
you	habláis	coméis	vivís
they	hablan	comen	viven

How to use the present tense

Use the present tense to talk about:

• what are you are doing NOW
• what you do REGULARLY
• what things are LIKE.

You can also use the present tense to talk about planned future events.

Mañana voy a España. Tomorrow I'm going to Spain.

Recognise and use a range of present tense time expressions, e.g.

ahora	now
hoy	today
en este momento	at this moment
los martes	on Tuesdays.

Stem-changing verbs

In stem-changing verbs, the vowel in the syllable before the infinitive ending changes in the singular and 3rd person plural. There are three common groups.

	o ➡ ue	e ➡ ie	e ➡ i
	poder to be able	querer to want	pedir to ask
I	puedo	quiero	pido
you	puedes	quieres	pides
he / she / it	puede	quiere	pide
we	podemos	queremos	pedimos
you	podéis	queréis	pedís
they	pueden	quieren	piden

Other examples of stem-changing verbs:

u/o ➡ ue	e ➡ ie
jugar ➡ juego play	empezar ➡ empiezo start
dormir ➡ duermo sleep	entender ➡ entiendo understand
volver ➡ vuelvo return	pensar ➡ pienso think
encontrar ➡ encuentro meet	preferir ➡ prefiero prefer

¿Quieres salir esta noche?
Do you want to go out tonight?

Rafa juega al tenis todos los días.
Rafa plays tennis every day.

Now try this

Complete the sentences using the present tense.

1 No .... música clásica. *escuchar (I)*
2 Mis padres .... inglés. *hablar*
3 Mi amigo .... al baloncesto conmigo. *jugar*
4 ¿............. ir al cine conmigo esta noche? *querer (you singular informal)*
5 Siempre .... fruta para estar sanos. *comer (we)*
6 Siempre .... dinero en la calle. *encontrar (they)*
7 ¿............. en el campo? *vivir (you plural informal)*
8 Mi hermano .... en su propio dormitorio. *dormir*

Had a look ☐   Nearly there ☐   Nailed it! ☐

Reflexives & irregulars

Reflexive verbs include a reflexive pronoun which refers back to the person doing the action.

Present tense (regular)

Reflexive verbs have the same endings as other present tense verbs but contain a reflexive pronoun. Some are also stem-changing verbs.

	lavarse to wash	vestirse to get dressed
I	me lavo	me visto
you	te lavas	te vistes
he / she	se lava	se viste
we	nos lavamos	nos vestimos
you	os laváis	os vestís
they	se lavan	se visten

In the infinitive form, the pronoun can be added to the end of the verb.

Voy a levantarme.   I'm going to get up.

Useful reflexive verbs

Reflexive verbs are particularly useful when you're talking about daily routine.

acostarse	Me acuesto.	I go to bed.
dormirse	Me duermo.	I go to sleep.
despertarse	Me despierto.	I wake up.
ducharse	Me ducho.	I have a shower.
levantarse	Me levanto.	I get up.
peinarse	Me peino.	I comb my hair.

Me visto.   Me cepillo los dientes.

The verbs ir and haber

These are irregular in the present tense.

	ir – to go	haber – to have
I	voy	he
you	vas	has
he / she / it	va	ha/hay
we	vamos	hemos
you	vais	habéis
they	van	han/hay

Other irregular verbs

Some verbs are irregular in the 'I' form only.

conducir	to drive	➡ conduzco
conocer	to know / meet	➡ conozco
dar	to give	➡ doy
hacer	to make / do	➡ hago
poner	to put	➡ pongo
saber	to know	➡ sé
salir	to go out	➡ salgo
tener	to have	➡ tengo
traer	to bring	➡ traigo

Now try this

1 Complete the sentences with the correct reflexive pronouns.

1 .... despierto temprano.

2 Mi hermano .... ducha a las siete.

3 Mañana voy a peinar .... antes de desayunar.

4 .... acostamos siempre a la misma hora.

5 ¿A qué hora .... levantas normalmente?

6 Mis padres .... duchan después de desayunar.

2 Unscramble the verbs and translate them into English.

1 zoncoco   ....   3 somav   ....   5 olgas   ....

2 goten   ....   4 gnoop   ....   6 oagrit   ....

Ser and estar

Spanish has two verbs meaning 'to be': ser and estar. Both are irregular – you need to know them well.

The present tense of ser

	ser – to be
I am	soy
you are	eres
he / she / it is	es
we are	somos
you are	sois
they are	son

Roberto es un chico feliz.
Roberto is a happy boy.

When to use ser

Use ser for PERMANENT things.

• nationality
Soy inglés.   I'm English.
• occupation
Es profesor.   He's a teacher.
• colour and size
Es rojo. Es pequeño.   It's red. It's small.
• personality
Son habladoras.   They're talkative.
• telling the time
Son las tres.   It's three o'clock.

The present tense of estar

	estar – to be
I am	estoy
you are	estás
he / she / it is	está
we are	estamos
you are	estáis
they are	están

Hoy Alicia está
aburridísima.
Alicia is really
bored today.

When to use estar

Use estar for TEMPORARY things and LOCATIONS.

• illness
Estoy enfermo.   I'm unwell.
• appearance (temporary)
Estás guapo.   You look handsome.
• feelings (temporary)
Estoy contento porque gané la lotería.
I'm happy because I won the lottery.
• location
Madrid está en   Madrid is in Spain.
España.

Watch out for this one!
ser listo   to be clever
estar listo   to be ready

Now try this

Complete the sentences with **ser** or **estar** in the present tense.

1 ¿Dónde .... la parada de autobuses?

2 Valencia .... grande e interesante.

3 Mi hermano .... abogado.

4 .... constipado. (I)

5 Las botas .... negras.

6 Mi mejor amiga .... escocesa.

7 Hoy mis amigos no .... contentos porque tienen una prueba.

8 María .... guapa esta noche con su vestido nuevo.

The gerund

Gerunds are '-ing' words. Use this page to review how they're formed and used.

The gerund

To form the gerund of regular verbs, replace the infinitive ending as follows:

hablar – hablando

comer – comiendo

vivir – viviendo

Common irregular gerunds:

caer	cayendo	falling
dormir	durmiendo	sleeping
leer	leyendo	reading
oír	oyendo	hearing
pedir	pidiendo	asking (for something)
poder	pudiendo	being able to
reír	riendo	laughing

Está jugando al fútbol.

He's playing football.

Uses of the gerund

You use the gerund:

• to give more information about how something was or is being done

e.g. Voy andando al instituto.

I go to school on foot.

• after ir (to go), seguir (to keep on) and continuar (to continue)

Sigo aprendiendo informática porque es útil.

I keep studying ICT because it's useful.

• to form the present continuous and imperfect continuous tenses (see below).

You can't always translate an '-ing' verb in English by the gerund in Spanish, e.g.

Aprender español es emocionante.

Learning Spanish is exciting.

Vamos a salir mañana.

We're leaving tomorrow.

Present continuous tense

The present continuous describes what is happening at this moment:

present tense of estar + the gerund

	estar – to be	gerund
I	estoy	
you	estás	haciendo
he / she / it	está	saliendo
we	estamos	durmiendo
you	estáis	riendo
they	están	

Estoy viendo la televisión. I'm watching TV.

Imperfect continous tense

This tense describes what was happening at a certain moment in the past:

imperfect tense of estar + the gerund

	estar – to be	gerund
I	estaba	
you	estabas	visitando
he / she / it	estaba	estudiando
we	estábamos	escribiendo
you	estabais	buscando
they	estaban	

Estaba leyendo.   I was reading.

Now try this

Rewrite the sentences using the present continuous tense. Write them again using the imperfect continuous.

1 Juego al tenis.

2 Escribo un correo electrónico.

3 Habla con mi amigo Juan.

4 Duerme en la cama.

5 Como cereales.

6 Tomo el sol en la playa

7 Navegan por internet.

8 ¿Cantas en tu habitación?

The preterite tense

The preterite tense is used to talk about completed actions in the past.

Preterite tense (regular)

To form the preterite tense of regular verbs, replace the infinitive ending as follows:

	hablar – to speak	comer – to eat	vivir – to live
I	hablé	comí	viví
you	hablaste	comiste	viviste
he / she / it	habló	comió	vivió
we	hablamos	comimos	vivimos
you	hablasteis	comisteis	vivisteis
they	hablaron	comieron	vivieron

Be careful – accents can be significant.
Hablo. I speak.
Habló. He / She spoke.

How to use the preterite tense

You use the preterite to describe completed actions in the past.

El año pasado viajé a Estados Unidos.
Last year I travelled to the United States.

Recognise and use a range of preterite tense time expressions,

ayer	yesterday
anoche	last night
anteayer / antes de ayer	the day before yesterday
el verano pasado	last summer
la semana pasada	last week

Preterite tense (irregular)

	ir – to go ser – to be	hacer – to do	ver – to see
yo	fui	hice	vi
tú	fuiste	hiciste	viste
él / ella	fue	hizo	vio
nosotros/as	fuimos	hicimos	vimos
vosotros/as	fuisteis	hicisteis	visteis
ellos/as	fueron	hicieron	vieron

The verbs **ir** and **ser** have the same forms in the preterite. Use context to work out which is meant.

Useful irregular preterite forms to know:

dar	di	I gave
estar	estuve	I was
saber	supe	I knew
andar	anduve	I walked
venir	vine	I came
poner	puse	I put
decir	dije	I said

Note these verbs with irregular spelling in 'I' form only:

tocar	toqué	I played
cruzar	crucé	I crossed
empezar	empecé	I started
jugar	jugué	I played
llegar	llegué	I arrived

Now try this

Identify the tense in each sentence (present or preterite). Then translate the sentences into English.

1 Voy a Italia.
2 Llegué a las seis.
3 Navego por Internet.
4 Escuchó música.
5 Fue a una fiesta que fue guay.
6 Hizo frío y llovió un poco.
7 Vimos a Pablo en el mercado.
8 Jugué al baloncesto en la playa.

The imperfect tense

The imperfect is another verb tense used to talk about the past.

Imperfect tense (regular)

To form the imperfect tense of regular verbs, replace the infinitive ending as follows:

	hablar – to speak	comer – to eat	vivir – to live
I	hablaba	comía	vivía
you	hablabas	comías	vivías
he / she / it	hablaba	comía	vivía
we	hablábamos	comíamos	vivíamos
you	hablabais	comíais	vivíais
they	hablaban	comían	vivían

-er and -ir verbs have the same endings.

Aim to use both the **imperfect** and the **preterite** in your work to aim for a higher grade.

How to use the imperfect tense

You use the imperfect to talk about:

* what people USED TO DO / how things USED TO BE

  Antes no separaba la basura.
  I didn't use to sort the rubbish before.

* REPEATED ACTIONS in the past

  Jugaba al tenis todos los días.
  I played tennis every day.

* DESCRIPTIONS in the past

  El hotel era caro.
  The hotel was expensive.

Cuidaba a niños. Ahora trabajo como jardinera.
I used to look after children. Now I work as a gardener.

Imperfect tense (irregular)

Only three verbs are irregular:

	ir – to go	ser – to be	ver – to see
I	iba	era	veía
you	ibas	eras	veías
he / she / it	iba	era	veía
we	íbamos	éramos	veíamos
you	ibais	erais	veíais
they	iban	eran	veían

Preterite or imperfect?

* Use the preterite tense for a SINGLE / COMPLETED event in the past.
* Use the imperfect tense for REPEATED / CONTINUOUS events in the past.

  En Brighton había un castillo.
  There used to be a castle in Brighton.

  Ayer visité Brighton.
  Yesterday I visited Brighton.

Now try this

Complete the sentences with the imperfect or preterite tense, as appropriate.

1 Mi madre .... para Iberia todos los veranos. *trabajar*

2 Ayer .... mucho chocolate. *comer* (I eat)

3 Antes .... a Grecia a menudo con mis padres. *ir* (I go)

4 En los años noventa .... menos paro que ahora. *haber*

5 El verano pasado .... latinoamérica por primera vez. *visitar* (I visit)

6 De pequeño mi hermanito .... siempre. *llorar*

The future tense

To aim for a higher grade, you need to use a future tense as well as the present and past.

Future tense

To form the future tense of most verbs, add the following endings to the infinitive:

ir – to go			
I	iré	we	iremos
you	irás	you	iréis
he / she / it	irá	they	irán

Some verbs use a different stem. You need to memorise these:

decir to say	➡	diré I will say
hacer to make / do	➡	haré I will make / do
poder to be able to	➡	podré I will be able to
querer to want	➡	querré I will want
saber to know	➡	sabré I will know
salir to leave	➡	saldré I will leave
tener to have	➡	tendré I will have
venir to come	➡	vendré I will come
haber there is / are	➡	habré there will be

Immediate future tense

You form the immediate future tense as follows:

present tense of ir + a + infinitive

	ir – to go		infinitive
I	voy		
you	vas		mandar
he / she / it	va	a	bailar
we	vamos		salir
you	vais		venir
they	van		

¿Vas a comer algo?
Are you going to have something to eat?

Vamos a ir a la fiesta.
We're going to go to the festival.

Recognise and use a range of time expressions that indicate the future, e.g. **mañana** tomorrow, **mañana por la mañana** tomorrow morning, **el mes que viene** next month, **el próximo viernes** next Friday.

Using the future tense

Use the future tense to talk about what WILL happen in the future.

El año que viene será difícil encontrar un buen trabajo.
Next year it will be difficult to find a good job.

Si trabajo como voluntario, mejoraré el mundo.
If I work as a volunteer, I will make the world better.

Using the immediate future tense

You use the immediate future tense to say what is going to happen. It is used to talk about future plans.

En Barcelona va a comprar recuerdos.
He's going to buy souvenirs in Barcelona.

Voy a salir esta tarde.
I'm going to leave this afternoon.

Now try this

1 Rewrite the sentences using the future tense.
   1 Nunca fumo.
   2 Ayudo a los demás.
   3 Cambiamos el mundo.
   4 Trabajo en un aeropuerto.

2 Rewrite these using the immediate future tense.
   1 Salgo a las seis.
   2 Soy médico.
   3 Va a España.
   4 Mañana juego al tenis.

The conditional

The conditional is used to describe what you WOULD DO or what WOULD HAPPEN in the future.

The conditional

To form the conditional, you add the following endings to the infinitive:

	hablar – to speak
I	hablaría
you	hablarías
he / she / it	hablaría
we	hablaríamos
you	hablaríais
they	hablarían

The endings are the same for ALL verbs.

Some verbs use a different stem.

decir to say	→	diría
hacer to do	→	haría
poder to be able to	→	podría
querer to want	→	querría
saber to know	→	sabría
salir to leave	→	saldría
tener to have	→	tendría
venir to come	→	vendría
haber there is / are	→	habría

Un sistema de alquiler de bicicletas sería una idea muy buena.
A bike hire scheme would be a really good idea.

Use **poder** in the conditional + the infinitive to say what you COULD do.
Podríamos ir a Ibiza.   We could go to Ibiza.

Use **deber** in the conditional + the infinitive to say what you SHOULD do.
Debería fumar menos cigarrillos.
I should smoke fewer cigarettes.

Expressing future intent

The conditional can be used to express future intent. Use gustar in the conditional + the infinitive.

En el futuro ...

me gustaría ir a Australia.
I'd love to go to Australia.

me gustaría ser bailarín.
I'd love to be a dancer.

me gustaría comprar un coche nuevo.
I'd like to buy a new car.

You can also use me encantaría, e.g. Me encantaría ser futbolista.

Now try this

Rewrite the text, changing the verbs in bold to the conditional.

Para mantenerme en forma **bebo** mucha agua. **Hago** mucho ejercicio y **practico** mucho deporte. Nunca **tomo** drogas y no **bebo** alcohol. **Como** mucha fruta y **me acuesto** temprano – siempre **duermo** ocho horas, gracias a eso **llevo** una vida sana.

Perfect and pluperfect

The perfect and pluperfect are two more tenses used to talk about the past. You should be able to use both.

Perfect tense

To form the perfect tense, use the present tense of haber + past participle:

	haber – to have
I	he
you	has
he/she/it	ha
we	hemos
you	habéis
they	han

Pluperfect tense

To form the pluperfect tense, use the imperfect tense of haber + past participle:

	haber – to have
I	había
you	habías
he/she/it	había
we	habíamos
you	habíais
they	habían

Past participle

To form the past participle, replace the infinitive ending as follows:

hablar – hablado

comer – comido

vivir – vivido

Ha comprado un CD nuevo.	He has bought a new CD.
No habían salido.	They hadn't gone out.
Había hecho mis deberes.	I had done my homework.
¿Has visto a María?	Have you seen María?

Here are some common irregular past participles:

abrir	abierto	➡	opened
decir	dicho	➡	said
escribir	escrito	➡	written
hacer	hecho	➡	done
poner	puesto	➡	put
romper	roto	➡	broken
ver	visto	➡	seen
volver	vuelto	➡	returned

Using the perfect tense

The perfect tense describes what someone HAS DONE or something that HAS HAPPENED.

He ido a la piscina.
I have been to the swimming pool.

Using the pluperfect tense

The pluperfect tense describes what someone HAD DONE or something that HAD HAPPENED at a particular time in the past.

Cuando llegó, el concierto había empezado ya.

When he arrived, the concert had already started.

Now try this

Rewrite the sentences in the correct order. Identify the tense in each one: perfect or pluperfect?

1 visitado / he / . / novio / mi / con / Palma
2 ayuda / hecho / deberes / mi / . / han / sus / con
3 ido / . / habíamos / Pablo / con / supermercado / al
4 amor / de / carta / una / . / escrito / ha / hermana / mi
5 has / ¿ / abrigo / mi / visto / ?
6 llegó / cuando / , / primos / ya / comido / . / mis / habían /

99

Giving instructions

You use the imperative to give INSTRUCTIONS and COMMANDS.

The imperative

The imperative has a different form depending on:

- who is receiving the command
- whether the command is positive or negative.

Formal commands use the 3rd person forms of the present subjunctive for both positive and negative.

POSITIVE IMPERATIVES (INFORMAL)

escuchar – to listen	correr – to run	abrir – to open
To one person: present tense –'you' singular minus s		
¡Escucha! Listen!	¡Corre! Run!	¡Abre! Open!
To more than one person: infinitive with final r changed to d		
¡Escuchad! Listen!	¡Corred! Run!	¡Abrid! Open!

NEGATIVE IMPERATIVES (INFORMAL)

To one person: present subjunctive – 'you' singular		
¡No escuches! Don't listen!	¡No corras! Don't run!	¡No abras! Don't open!
To more than one person: present subjunctive – 'you' plural		
¡No escuchéis! Don't listen!	¡No corráis! Don't run!	¡No abráis! Don't open!

Irregular imperatives

These verbs have irregular imperatives in the 'you' singular form.

decir	➡	¡Di!	Say!
hacer	➡	¡Haz!	Do!
ir	➡	¡Ve!	Go!
dar	➡	¡Da!	Give!
salir	➡	¡Sal!	Leave!
tener	➡	¡Ten!	Have!

How to use the imperative

The imperative is used to give commands and instructions.

Toma la primera calle a la izquierda.
Take the first street on the left.

Poned la mesa, por favor.
Set the table, please.

¡No hables!
Don't talk!

Now try this

Translate the instructions into English.

1 Escríbeme.
2 Espera a tu hermana.
3 No me digas.
4 ¡No gritéis!
5 Haz clic aquí.
6 ¡No saques fotos!
7 Contestad las preguntas.
8 No dejes todo para último momento.

¡No saques fotos!

The present subjunctive

The subjunctive form of the verb is used in certain constructions.

The present subjunctive

To form the present subjunctive, replace the -o ending of the 'I' form of the present tense as follows:

	hablar to speak	comer to eat	vivir to live
I	hable	coma	viva
you	hables	comas	vivas
he / she / it	hable	coma	viva
we	hablemos	comamos	vivamos
you	habléis	comáis	viváis
they	hablen	coman	vivan

-er and -ir verbs have the same endings.

This rule works for most verbs which are irregular in the present tense.

Infinitive	Present	Subjunctive
hacer	hago	haga
tener	tengo	tenga

Two verbs, ir and ser, are different.

	ir – to go	ser – to be
I	vaya	sea
you	vayas	seas
he / she / it	vaya	sea
we	vayamos	seamos
you	vayáis	seáis
they	vayan	sean

Remember: the subjunctive is also used in some imperatives – see page 100.

How to use the subjunctive

The subjunctive is used:

* to express doubt or uncertainty

No creo que tenga tiempo.
I don't think I have time.

* to express a negative opinion

No es verdad que sea adicto al ordenador.
It isn't true that I'm a computer addict.

* after ojalá

¡Ojalá (que) nadie me vea!
Let's hope no one sees me!

* after cuando when talking about the future

Cuando sea mayor, quiero hacer caída libre.
When I'm older, I want to do skydiving.

* to express a wish with querer que (with a change of subject)

¿Quieres que nos vayamos?
Do you want us to go?

* with certain phrases

Es importante que estemos en forma.
It is important that we are fit.

Es esencial que te despiertes temprano.

Now try this

Translate the sentences into English.
1 Cuando vaya a la universidad, estudiaré francés.
2 No creo que tu amigo sea guapo.
3 Cuando tenga dieciocho años, me tomaré un año sabático.
4 Quiero que hables con Pablo.
5 No es verdad que la comida inglesa sea horrible.
6 No creo que Italia sea el mejor equipo de fútbol.

It's important you can **recognise** the subjunctive. If you're really aiming high, you could also try to **use** a few subjunctive forms in your writing and speaking.

Negatives

You need to be able to understand and use negatives in all parts of the exam.

Negatives

no	not
no … nada	nothing / not anything
no … nunca	never
no … jamás	never
no … ni … ni …	not … (either) … or …
no … tampoco	not … either
no … ningún / ninguna	no / not any
no … nadie	no one

No tengo nada que ponerme.
I don't have anything to wear.

No quiero ni nadar ni hacer yoga.
I don't want to swim or do yoga.

No me gustan los perros tampoco.
I don't like dogs either.

How to use negatives

- The simplest way to make a sentence negative in Spanish is to use no. It comes before the verb.

  No nadé en el mar.
  I didn't swim in the sea.

- Negative expressions with two parts sandwich the verb (i.e. they go round it).

  Dicen que no nieva nunca en Málaga.
  They say that it never snows in Malaga.

- Two-part negative expressions can be shortened and put before the verb for emphasis.

  Nadie está aquí. No one's here.

Expressions to use with negatives

Ya no estudio alemán.	I no longer study German.
No bebo agua sino zumo de naranja.	I don't drink water but orange juice.
Todavía no ha estudiado mucho.	He hasn't studied a lot yet.
Espero que no.	I hope not.
Creo que no.	I don't think so.
Claro que no.	Of course not.

Use a range of negatives in your Spanish to aim for a higher grade.

Now try this

Make the sentences negative, giving the opposite meanings.

1 Siempre como verduras.
2 Tengo un libro.
3 Conozco a todos sus amigos.
4 Todo el mundo juega a pelota.
5 Siempre hago mis deberes.
6 Me gusta navegar por Internet y descargar música.
7 Tiene todo.
8 Tengo muchos amigos en Londres.

Special verbs

Verbs like gustar are used mainly in the 3rd person. You'll need them for a lot of topics, so they're worth learning carefully.

Present tense of gustar

Me gusta ('I like') literally translates as 'it pleases me'. The thing that does the pleasing (i.e. the thing I like) is the subject.

Me gusta este libro.   I like this book.

If the subject is plural, use me gustan.

Me gustan estos libros.   I like these books.

The pronoun changes as follows:

me	gusta(n)	I like
te	gusta(n)	you like
le	gusta(n)	he / she / it likes
nos	gusta(n)	we like
os	gusta(n)	you like
les	gusta(n)	they like

encantar behaves in the same way as gustar:
Le encanta la música rock. He loves rock music.

Preterite tense of gustar

In the preterite:

me gusta ➡ me gustó

me gustan ➡ me gustaron

The pronouns in the other forms are the same as for the present tense.

Nos gustó la comida española.
We liked Spanish food.

Le gustaron las tiendas.
She liked the shops.

To talk about other people's likes/dislikes, you need a before their name:

A Ignacio le gusta el deporte. Ignacio likes sport.

If you're aiming for higher grades, use gustar in the preterite to extend your language range.

Other verbs like gustar

Other verbs follow the same pattern as gustar: pronoun + 3rd person singular/plural of the verb

doler	me duelen(n)	My ... hurt(s)
quedar	me queda(n)	I have ... left
hacer falta	me hace(n) falta	I need ...
faltar	me falta(n)	I'm missing ...

Me duele el tobillo.
My ankle hurts.

Les quedan 20 euros.
They have 20 euros left.

¿Te hace falta una cuchara?
Do you need a spoon?

Le faltan dos libros.
He's missing two books.

Now try this

Complete the sentences.

1 .... el brazo. *(doler, I)*

2 .... el queso. *(gustar, she)*

3 .... los españoles. *(gustar, I, preterite)*

4 .... un cuchillo. *(hacer falta, they)*

5 .... los pies. *(doler, he)*

6 .... el español. *(encantar, I)*

7 .... cinco euros. *(quedar, we)*

8 .... las películas francesas. *(gustar, María)*

Por and para

Por and para are both often translated by 'for' in English. Learn the different contexts in which they're used.

Using por

You use por for:

① CAUSE
Pagué cien euros por el vuelo.
I paid €100 for the flight.

El vuelo está cancelado por la huelga.
The flight was cancelled because of the strike.

② to indicate action ON BEHALF OF someone
Lo hizo por mí. She did it for me.

③ when expressing RATES
Gano seis euros por hora.
I earn €6 per hour.

④ periods of TIME
Me quedaré en Barcelona por poco tiempo.
I will stay in Barcelona for a short time.

⑤ means of COMMUNICATION
Me llamó por teléfono.
He called me on the phone.

Using para

You use para for:

① PURPOSE (it can often be translated by 'in order to')
Llevamos una botella de agua fría para el viaje.
We're taking a bottle of cold water for the journey.

Voy a utilizar mi tarjeta de crédito para pagar el hotel.
I'm going to use my credit card to pay for the hotel.

Voy a comprar unos regalos para mi familia.
I'm going to buy some presents for my family.

② DESTINATION
Ha salido para Bilbao.
She has left for Bilbao.

③ periods of TIME in the future
Quisiera una habitación para quince días.
I would like a room for a fortnight.

Try writing out phrases with **por** and **para**, using one colour for **por** each time and another colour for **para**. Then when you're trying to remember which one to use, try to visualise the colour.

Now try this

1 Choose **por** or **para** to complete these sentences.

1 Voy a ir a Madrid .... hacer compras.

2 El tren .... Sevilla sale a las seis.

3 Gracias .... el regalo.

4 Los deberes son .... mañana.

5 Este regalo es .... mi profesor.

6 Voy a llamarle .... teléfono.

7 Una azafata gana veinte euros .... hora.

2 Tick the sentences which are correct. Correct those that are wrong.

1 Salimos por Nueva York.

2 Solo estudio para la mañana.

3 Por ganar hay que trabajar duro.

4 Voy a hacerlo para ti.

5 Juego al fútbol para divertirme.

6 Estas flores son por mi novia.

7 Ganar dinero para vender tu móvil viejo.

8 En 18 por ciento de las casas hay una motocicleta.

Questions and exclamations

Being able to use questions and exclamations is essential in most topics.

How to ask questions

To ask yes/no questions, use the same language as you would to say the sentence and:

• if you're writing, add question marks

• if you're speaking, use a rising intonation at the end.

¿Estudias español?

Do you study Spanish?

¿Quieres ir al polideportivo?

Do you want to go to the leisure centre?

> Remember the ¿ at the start.

To ask open questions, use a question word.

¿Cuándo?	When?
¿Dónde?	Where?
¿Adónde?	Where to?
¿De dónde?	From where?
¿Cuánto/a?	How much?
¿Cuántos/as?	How many?
¿Qué?	What?
¿Por qué?	Why?
¿Cómo?	How?
¿Cuál(es)?	Which (ones)?
¿Quién(es)?	Who?
¿Cuál (de estos libros) te gusta más?	Which (one of these books) do you like more?

> Don't forget the accents on question words.

Using exclamations

Using exclamations is a good way to extend how you give opinions in your spoken and written Spanish. Here are some useful examples:

¡Qué lástima!	What a shame!
¡Qué problema!	What a problem!
¡Qué raro!	How strange!
¡Qué va!	No way!
¡Qué rollo!	How boring!

> Remember the ¡ at the start as well as at the end.

¡Qué emocionante!
How exciting!

¡Qué difícil!
How difficult!

Question tag

English has a lot of different ways of asking for confirmation, e.g. 'doesn't he?', 'haven't they?', 'can't you?'. In Spanish it's much easier. You just put verdad at the end of a question.

¿Pablo es tu novio, verdad?

Pablo is your boyfriend, isn't he?

Now try this

Match the sentence halves.

1 ¿Cuál   a cuesta?
2 ¿Adónde   b personas hay en tu clase?
3 ¿Quién   c te llamas?
4 ¿Dónde   d es tu asignatura preferida?
5 ¿Cuánto   e está Jaén?
6 ¿Cuántas   f fuiste de vacaciones el año pasado?
7 ¿Cómo   g es tu cumpleaños?
8 ¿Cuándo   h es tu pintor preferido?

Connectives and adverbs

Use connectives to link phrases and sentences, and use adverbs to add detail to your Spanish.

Connectives

Connectives are words that link phrases and sentences together. You can use them to make your Spanish more varied and interesting.

Hago atletismo pero no me gusta mucho.

I do athletics but I don't like it much.

además	as well / besides
antes (de)	before
así que	so / therefore
después (de)	after
entonces	then
mientras	while
o	or
pero	but
porque	because
dado que	given that
por eso	therefore
por una parte	on the one hand
por otra parte	on the other hand
pues	then
si	if
sin embargo	however
también	also
y	and

Another good way to improve your work is to extend your sentences using clauses with: **que** that / who, **donde** where, **cuando** when, **como** like / as, **cuyo** whose.

Adverbs

Adverbs describe how an action is done – they give you more detail about verbs.

They are formed by adding –mente to the feminine form of the adjective

lento ➡ lenta ➡ lentamente slowly

Adverbs usually come AFTER the verb.

Monta a caballo frecuentemente.
She goes riding frequently.

Sometimes they come BEFORE the verb, for emphasis.

Siempre nado los martes.
I always go swimming on Tuesdays.

Irregular adverbs

Here are some useful irregular adverbs to learn:

bastante	enough	despacio	slow
bien	well	mal	badly
demasiado	too	mucho	a lot
	much	poco	a little
deprisa	fast	ya	already

1 Connect the sentence pairs with an appropriate connective.
  1 Nunca voy a Paris. Es aburrido.
  2 Jugaba al baloncesto. Juan hacía patinaje.
  3 Estudiar. Iré a la universidad.
  4 Nos gustaría ir a la playa. Está lloviendo.

2 Make adverbs from the adjectives. Translate them into English.
  1 tranquilo
  2 perfecto
  3 difícil
  4 severo

Numbers

Numbers come up in almost EVERY context. Make sure you know them well.

Numbers

1	uno	11	once	21	veintiuno	100	cien
2	dos	12	doce	22	veintidós	101	ciento uno
3	tres	13	trece	30	treinta	200	doscientos/as
4	cuatro	14	catorce	31	treinta y uno	333	trescientos/as
5	cinco	15	quince	32	treinta y dos		treinta y tres
6	seis	16	dieciséis	40	cuarenta	1000	mil
7	siete	17	diecisiete	50	cincuenta		
8	ocho	18	dieciocho	60	sesenta		
9	nueve	19	diecinueve	70	setenta		
10	diez	20	veinte	80	ochenta		
				90	noventa		

> The hundreds need to agree. Note: there are some irregular forms: 500 – **quinientos**, 700 – **setecientos**, 900 – **novecientos**.

> The pattern for 31, 32, etc., is the same for 41, 42, etc.

Ordinal numbers

When used with nouns, ordinal numbers agree.

primero	first	sexto	sixth
segundo	second	séptimo	seventh
tercero	third	octavo	eighth
cuarto	fourth	noveno	ninth
quinto	fifth	décimo	tenth

Primero and tercero change to primer and tercer before a masculine singular noun, e.g. el tercer día.

> Ordinals are NOT used for dates except for the 1st.

Telling the time

Son las cinco.	It's five o'clock.
A las diez.	At ten o'clock.

> One o'clock is different: Es la una.

3.05	las tres y cinco
3.15	las tres y cuarto
3.30	las tres y media
3.45	las cuatro menos cuarto
3.55	las cuatro menos cinco

Dates

Dates follow this pattern:

13 December 1978 =

el trece de diciembre de mil novecientos setenta y ocho

> You don't use a capital letter for the months.

The first of the month can be either: el primero de abril or el uno de abril.

Now try this

Write the numbers, dates and times in Spanish.

1 8.40   **2** 465   **3** 12 June 2014   **4** 7th   **5** 11.30   **6** 76   **7** 1 January 1997   **8** 3rd

Vocabulary

These pages cover key Spanish vocabulary that you need to know. This section starts with general terms that are useful in a wide variety of situations and then divides into vocabulary for each of the four main topics covered in this revision guide:

1 General vocabulary   **2** Lifestyle   **3** Leisure

4 Home and environment   **5** Work and education

F Sections to be learnt by all candidates   **H** Sections to be learnt by Higher candidates only

Learning vocabulary is essential preparation for your reading and listening exams. Don't try to learn too much at once – concentrate on learning and testing yourself on a page at a time.

1 General vocabulary

Comparisons

Comparatives and superlatives of adjectives and adverbs

bastante	quite
bien	well
demasiado	too, too much
descripción (f)	description
igual que	like, the same as
más (que)	more (than)
máximo	maximum
mayor	bigger
mayoría (f)	majority
mejor	better
menor	less, smaller
menos (que)	less (than)
mínimo	minimum
mismo	same
muy	very
parecido a	similar to
peor	worse
poco (e.g. poco ruidoso)	little (e.g. a little noisy)
por ejemplo	for example
tan ... como	as ... as
tanto ... como	as much ... as
comparar	to compare

Conjunctions

a pesar de	despite
así que	so
aun (si)	even (if)
aunque	even though
como	as, since
cuando	when
incluso	even
mientras (que)	whereas
o / u	or

pero	but
por eso	that's why
por lo tanto	therefore
porque	because
pues	since, because
si	if
sin embargo	however
tal vez	perhaps, maybe
también	also
y / e	and
ya (que)	since

Connectives

además	also
aparte de	apart from
claro que	clearly
dado que	given that
es decir	that is to say
por un lado / por otro lado	on one hand / the other
por una parte / por otra parte	on one hand / the other
sin duda	without doubt

Prepositions

a	at, to
con	with
de	from, of
en	in, on
hacia	towards
hasta	until
para	for, in order to
por	for, by
según	according to
sin	without

Negatives

jamás	never
ni ... ni	neither ... nor
nada	nothing
nadie	no one

ninguno	none
no	not
nunca	never
sino	except
tampoco	neither
ya no	no longer

The important verbs

acabar de (+ inf.)	to finish
dar	to give
deber	to have to, must
estar	to be
hacer	to do, to make
hacerse	to become
hay	there is, there are
hay que	we / you must
ir	to go
ir a (+ inf.)	to be going to
irse	to leave
ocurrir	to happen
oír	to hear
pasar	to happen
poder	to be able, can
poner	to put
querer	to want, to love
quisiera	I would like
ser	to be
soler	to be in the habit of, usually
tener	to have
tener lugar	to take place
tener que	to have to
volverse	to become

Other expressions

unos (diez)	about (ten)
docena (f)	dozen
par (m)	pair
número (m)	number

Now try this

Practise connectives and prepositions by covering up the English column and then writing down the English translations yourself. Compare your answers with the list above. How many have you got right?

1 General vocabulary

Asking questions

Question words

¿Adónde?	Where to?
¿Cómo?	How?
¿Cuál(es)?	Which?
¿Cuándo?	When?
¿Cuánto?	How much?
¿Cuántos ...?	How many?
¿De dónde?	Where ... from?
¿De quién?	Whose?
¿Dónde?	Where?
¿Por dónde?	Whereabouts?
¿Por qué?	Why?
¿Qué?	What?
¿Quién?	Who?

Common questions

¿A qué hora?	At what time?
¿Cuánto cuesta(n)?	How much does it (do they) cost?
¿Cuánto es?	How much is it?
¿Cuánto vale(n)?	How much is it (are they) worth?
¿Cuántos años tiene(s)?	How old are you?
¿De qué color?	What colour?
¿Dónde está?	Where is it?
¿Para / Por cuánto tiempo?	How long?
¿Qué día?	What day?
¿Qué fecha?	What date?
¿Qué hora es?	What time is it?

Greetings and exclamations

¡Basta!	Enough!
¡Bienvenido!	Welcome!
¡Buen viaje!	Have a good trip / journey!
¡Buena suerte!	Good luck!
¡Claro!	Of course!
¡Cuidado!	Be careful!
¡Enhorabuena!	Congratulations!
¡Felices Pascuas!	Happy Easter!
¡Felices vacaciones!	Happy holidays!
¡Felicidades!	Congratulations!
¡Felicitaciones!	Congratulations!
¡Feliz Año Nuevo!	Happy New Year!

¡Feliz cumpleaños!	Happy birthday!
¡Feliz Navidad!	Happy Christmas!
¡Feliz santo!	Happy saint's day!
¡Ojo!	Look out!
¡Que aproveche!	Enjoy your meal!
¡Que lo pase(s) bien!	Have a good time!
¡Qué asco!	Yuk!
¡Qué bien!	Great!
¡Qué (+ adj.)!	How ...!
¡Qué horror!	How horrible!
¡Qué (+ noun)!	What a ...!
¡Qué lástima!	What a pity!
¡Qué pena!	What a shame!
¡Qué va!	Come on!
¡Socorro!	Help!
¿Cómo está(s)?	How are you?
¿De veras?	Really?
¿Qué hay?	What's up?
¿Qué pasa?	What's happening?
¿Qué tal?	How are you?
Adiós	Goodbye
Atentamente	Yours sincerely / faithfully
Buenas noches	Goodnight
Buenas tardes	Good evening
Buenos días	Good morning
Con permiso	Excuse me
De nada	You're welcome
Encantado	Pleased to meet you
Gracias	Thanks
Hasta el (lunes)	See you on (Monday)
Hasta luego	See you
Hasta mañana	See you tomorrow
Hasta pronto	See you soon
Hola	Hi
Lo siento	I'm sorry
Mucho gusto	Pleased to meet you
Perdón	Sorry
Perdone	Excuse me
Por favor	Please
Saludos	Best wishes
Sí	Yes

| Vale | OK |
| saludar | to greet |

Opinions

aburrido/a	boring
aceptable	acceptable
afortunado/a	lucky
agradable	pleasant
antiguo/a	old
apropiado/a	suitable
barato/a	cheap
bonito/a	pretty
bueno/a	good
calidad (f)	quality
caro/a	expensive
decepcionado/a	disappointed
decepcionante	disappointing
desafortunadamente	unfortunately
desagradable	disagreeable
desventaja (f)	disadvantage
diferencia (f)	difference
diferente	different
difícil	difficult
dificultad (f)	difficulty
distinto/a	different
divertido/a	amusing, enjoyable
duro/a	hard, difficult
económico/a	economical
emocionante	exciting
encantador(a)	enchanting, lovely
entretenido/a	entertaining
especial	special
espléndido/a	splendid
estupendo/a	marvellous, great
estúpido/a	stupid
excelente	excellent
extraordinario/a	extraordinary
fácil	easy
famoso/a	famous
fantástico/a	fantastic
fascinante	fascinating
fatal	terrible
favorable	favourable
favorito/a	favourite
fenomenal	great, terrific
feo/a	ugly
genial	brilliant, great

Now try this

Choose ten positive opinion words and ten negative ones. Memorise them. Then test yourself to see if you can spell them correctly.

① General vocabulary

hermoso/a	beautiful, handsome	dudar	to doubt	agosto	August
horroroso/a	horrible	encantar	to delight	se(p)tiembre	September
ideal	ideal	esperar	to hope	octubre	October
importante	important	estar de acuerdo	to agree	noviembre	November
imposible	impossible	estar a favor	to be in favour	diciembre	December
impresionante	impressive	estar en contra	to be against		
increíble	incredible	estar harto de	to be fed up with		

The clock

inseguro/a	insecure	fascinar	to fascinate	a eso de	around
interesante	interesting	fastidiar	to annoy	a tiempo	on time
inútil	useless	gustar	to please	en punto	exactly
mal	badly	interesarse	to be interested	exactamente	exactly
malo/a	bad			hora (f)	hour, time
maravilloso/a	marvellous	justificar	to justify	horario (m)	timetable
moderno/a	modern	odiar	to hate	media hora (f)	half-hour
negativo/a	negative	opinar	to think	medianoche (f)	midnight
nuevo/a	new	parecer	to seem	mediodía (m)	midday
perfecto/a	perfect	pasarlo bien / mal	to have a good / bad time	menos / y ...	... to / past
posible	possible			menos cuarto	quarter to
positivo/a	positive	pensar	to think	minuto (m)	minute
precioso/a	lovely	ponerse de acuerdo	to agree	segundo (m)	second
preferido/a	preferred			y cuarto	quarter past
profundo/a	deep	preferir	to prefer	y media	half past

Other time expressions (A–D)

raro/a	rare, odd	quedar en	to agree to	a diario	daily
regular	regular, average	querer decir	to mean	a fines de	at the end of
ridículo/a	ridiculous	reconocer	to recognise	a mediados de	in the middle of
seguro/a	safe	sentir(se)	to feel	a menudo	often
sencillo/a	simple	valer la pena	to be worthwhile	a partir de	since
sorprendido/a	surprised			aproximadamente	approximately

Expressions of time

típico/a	typical			a veces	sometimes
tonto/a	silly			ahora	now
tranquilo/a	calm			al mismo tiempo	at the same time

Days of the week

único/a	only, unique	lunes (m)	Monday	algunas veces	sometimes
útil	useful	martes (m)	Tuesday	anoche	last night
ventaja (f)	advantage	miércoles (m)	Wednesday	año (m)	year
viejo/a	old	jueves (m)	Thursday	antes (de)	before
aburrirse	to be / get bored	viernes (m)	Friday	ayer	yesterday
adorar	to adore	sábado (m)	Saturday	breve	short
apreciar	to appreciate	domingo (m)	Sunday	cada (x) días / horas	every (x) days / hours

The seasons

aprovechar(se)	to make use of	primavera (f)	spring	casi	nearly
alegrar(se)	to cheer up	verano (m)	summer	de ... a ...	from ... to
creer	to believe	otoño (m)	autumn	de momento	at the moment
dar igual	to be the same	invierno (m)	winter	de nuevo	again
decepcionar	to disappoint			de repente	suddenly

Months of the year

decir	to say	enero	January	de vez en cuando	from time to time
desear	to want	febrero	February	dentro de (dos horas)	within (two hours)
detestar	to hate	marzo	March		
disfrutar	to enjoy	abril	April	desde	from
divertirse	to have a good time	mayo	May	desde hace	since
		junio	June	después	after, since
		julio	July		

Now try this

Practise days and months by translating the birthdays of family and friends into Spanish.

General vocabulary

Other time expressions (D–Z)

día (m)	day
día festivo (m)	public holiday
día laborable (m)	working day
diariamente	daily
durante	during
durar	to last
en ese / este momento	at that / this moment
en seguida	at once
entonces	then
estación (f)	season
fecha (f)	date
fin de semana (m)	weekend
final (m)	end
finalmente	finally
frecuente	frequent
futuro/a	future
futuro (m)	future
generalmente	generally
hace (dos años)	(two years) ago
hoy	today
inmediatamente	immediately
los lunes, etc.	on Mondays, etc.
luego	then
mañana	tomorrow
mes (m)	month
mientras tanto	meanwhile
momento (m)	moment
mucho tiempo	a lot of time
noche (f)	night
normalmente	usually
otra vez	again
pasado (m)	past
pasado/a	last
pasado mañana	the day after tomorrow
permanente	permanent
pocas veces	seldom
por año	a year (of e.g. times)
por fin	finally
por lo general	in general
porvenir (m)	future
principio (m)	beginning
pronto	soon
próximo/a	next
... que viene (el mes, etc.)	next (month, etc.)
quince días	fortnight
rápido/a	quick
raramente	rarely
rato (m)	time
reciente(mente)	recent(ly)
semana (f)	week
siempre	always
siglo (m)	century
siguiente	following
sobre	on (top of)
solamente	only
sólo/a	only
tardar	to be late
tarde	late
tarde (f)	afternoon, evening
temprano	early
tener prisa	to be in a hurry
tiempo (m)	time
todas las semanas	every week
todavía	still, yet
todos los días	every
últimamente	finally
último/a	last
vez (f) (pl. veces)	time(s)
volver a	to resume

Location and distance

a un paso (de)	near
abajo	below
adelante	forward
afuera	outside
ahí	there
aislado/a	isolated
al final (de)	at the end (of)
allá	(over) there
allí	there
alrededor (de)	around
aquí	here
arriba	above
atrás	behind
céntrico/a	central
centro (m)	centre
cerca (de)	near
contra	against
debajo (de)	under
delante (de)	in front (of)
dentro (de)	inside
derecha (f) (a la)	right (on the)
derecho/a	straight
detrás (de)	behind

dirección (f)	direction
distancia (f)	distance
en / por todas partes	everywhere
en las afueras	on the outskirts
encima (de)	on
enfrente (de)	opposite
entre	between
este (m)	east
exterior (m)	outside
fondo (m)	background, bottom
fuera (de)	outside
interior (m)	interior
izquierda (f) (a la)	left (on the)
kilómetro (m)	kilometre
lado (m) (al ... de)	side (beside)
lejos (de)	far (from)
lugar (m)	place
medio (m) (de)	middle (of)
metro (m)	metre
norte (m)	north
oeste (m)	west
sitio (m)	place
sur (m)	south
todo recto	straight ahead
estar situado/a	to be situated
encontrarse	to be situated
estar a ... (kilómetros / minutos) de	to be ... (kilometres / minutes) away from

Colours

amarillo	yellow
azul	blue
blanco	white
claro	light
color (m)	colour
gris	grey
marrón	brown
morado	purple
naranja	orange
negro	black
oscuro	dark
pálido	pale
rojo	red
rosa	pink
rosado	pink
verde	green
violeta	violet
vivo	vivid, bright

Now try this

Cover up the English vocabulary above and make a note of any Spanish words you don't recognise. Learn these words, then try again in a week's time and see how many words you still don't recognise.

① General vocabulary

Weights and measures

alcanzar	to reach
alto/a	tall
altura (f)	height
ancho/a	wide
ancho (m)	width
bajo/a	low, short
bolsa (f)	bag
bote (m)	tin
botella (f)	bottle
caja (f)	box
cantidad (f)	quantity
cartón (m)	carton
centímetro (m)	centimetre
completo/a	full
cuarto (m)	quarter
delgado/a	thin
doble (m)	double
estrecho/a	narrow
gordo/a	fat
gramo (m)	gram
grande	big
grueso/a	thick
lata (f)	can
litro (m)	litre
lleno/a	full
mediano/a	medium
medida (f)	measurement
medio/a	half
mitad (f)	half
mucho/a	a lot of
paquete (m)	packet
pedazo (m)	piece
pequeño/a	small
peso (m)	weight
poco (un)	(a) little
ración (f)	portion
suficiente	enough
talla (f)	height
tamaño (m)	size
trozo (m)	piece
vacío/a	empty
bastar	to be enough
medir	to measure
pesar	to weigh

Shape

cuadrado/a	square
forma (f)	shape
redondo/a	round

Weather

buen / mal tiempo	good / bad weather
caliente	hot, warm
calor (m)	heat
caluroso/a	hot, warm
chubasco (m)	shower
cielo (m)	sky
clima (m)	climate
despejado/a	clear
estable	stable
fresco/a	fresh
frío (m)	cold
grado (m)	degree
hielo (m)	ice
húmedo/a	damp
lluvia (f)	rain
niebla (f)	fog
nieve (f)	snow
nube (f)	cloud
nublado/a	cloudy
nuboso/a	cloudy
pronóstico (m)	forecast
relámpago (m)	lightning
seco/a	dry
sol (m)	sun
sombra (f)	shade
temperatura (f)	temperature
templado/a	mild
tiempo (m)	weather
tormenta (f)	storm
tormentoso/a	stormy
trueno (m)	thunder
viento (m)	wind
hacer (frío)	to be (cold)
helar	to freeze
llover	to rain
mojar(se)	to (get) wet
nevar	to snow
tener (calor)	to be (hot)

Access

abierto/a	open
abrir	to open
acceso (m)	access
cerrado/a	closed
cerrar	to close
gratis	free (of charge)
gratuito/a	free
hacer falta	to be necessary
libre	free
necesario/a	necessary
ocupado/a	engaged, occupied
permitir	to permit
prohibido/a	prohibited, forbidden
prohibir	to prohibit, forbid

Correctness

cierto/a	certain
correcto/a	correct
equivocado/a	wrong
exacto/a	exact
falso/a	false
falta (f)	error
mentira (f)	lie
mentiroso/a	lying
razón (f)	reason
verdad (f)	truth
verdadero/a	true
corregir	to correct
estar equivocado/a	to be wrong
mentir	to lie
tener razón	to be right

Materials

algodón (m)	cotton
cerámica (f)	ceramic
cristal (m)	glass, crystal
cuero (m)	leather
lana (f)	wool
madera (f)	wood
oro (m)	gold
papel (m)	paper
piel (f)	leather, skin
plástico (m)	plastic
plata (f)	silver
seda (f)	silk
tela (f)	fabric, cloth
vidrio (m)	glass

Now try this

Choose ten weather expressions from the weather section on this page. Learn them then try to write the Spanish from memory, with the correct spellings. Check back and try again with any you got wrong.

② Lifestyle

Health (A–R)

a la plancha	grilled
aceite (m)	oil
adictivo/a	addictive
adicto/a (m/f)	addict
agua (f)	water
agua mineral (con / sin gas) (f)	mineral water (still / sparkling)
ajo (m)	garlic
alcohólico/a	alcoholic
alimento (m)	food
arroz (m)	rice
asado/a	roast(ed)
atún (m)	tuna
azúcar (m)	sugar
bacalao (m)	cod
barra (de pan) (f)	baguette
bebida (f)	drink
bien hecho	well done (meat)
bisté (m)	steak
bistec (m)	steak
bocadillo (m)	sandwich
bombón (m)	chocolate
borracho/a	drunk
café (m)	coffee
calamares (mpl)	squid
cansado/a	tired
caramelo (m)	sweet, caramel
carne (f)	meat
cena (f)	evening meal
cereales (mpl)	cereal
cerveza (f)	beer
chocolate (m)	chocolate
chorizo (m)	spicy sausage, chorizo
chuleta (f)	chop, cutlet
churros (mpl)	fritters
cigarrillo (m)	cigarette
cocaína (f)	cocaine
cocina (f)	cookery, cuisine
col (f)	cabbage
coliflor (f)	cauliflower
comida (f)	meal, food, lunch
comida basura (f)	junk food
comida rápida (f)	fast food

corazón (m)	heart
cuerpo (m)	body
de cerdo	pork
de cordero	lamb
de ternera	veal
de vaca	beef
depresión (f)	depression
desayuno (m)	breakfast
dieta (f)	diet
dolor (m)	pain
droga (blanda / dura) (f)	drug (soft / hard)
dulce	sweet
ejercicio (físico) (m)	(physical) exercise
enfermedad (f)	illness
enfermo/a	sick
ensalada (f)	salad
entrenamiento (m)	training
espaguetis (mpl)	spaghetti
farmacia (f)	pharmacy
filete (m)	fillet
flan (m)	caramel custard
fresa (f)	strawberry
frito/a	fried
fruta (f)	fruit
fumador/a (m/f)	smoker
galleta (f)	biscuit
gambas (fpl)	prawns
gazpacho (m)	gazpacho, cold soup
grasa (f)	fat
hábito (m)	habit
hamburguesa (f)	hamburger
helado (m)	ice cream
huevo (m)	egg
humo (m)	smoke
inyección (f)	injection
jamón (de york) (m)	(cooked) ham
jamón serrano (m)	(cured) ham
judías verdes (fpl)	green beans
leche (f)	milk
lechuga (f)	lettuce
legumbres (fpl)	vegetables
limón (m)	lemon
limonada (f)	lemonade
mantequilla (f)	butter

manzana (f)	apple
mariscos (mpl)	seafood
melocotón (m)	peach
merienda (f)	snack
mermelada (f)	marmalade
muerto/a	dead
naranja (f)	orange
naranjada (f)	orangeade
nata (f)	cream
nuez (f)	nut, walnut
paella (f)	paella
pan (m)	bread
pasta (f)	pasta
pastel (m)	cake
patatas fritas (fpl)	chips, crisps
pera (f)	pear
perrito caliente (m)	hot dog
pescado (m)	fish
picante	spicy
pimienta (f)	(black) pepper
piña (f)	pineapple
plátano (m)	banana
pollo (m)	chicken
pulmones (mpl)	lungs
queso (m)	cheese
rehabilitación (f)	rehabilitation
rico/a	tasty

 zanahoria (f)

 champiñones (mpl)

 cebolla (f)

 guisantes (mpl)

 pimiento (m) (verde/rojo)

 patata (f)

 tomate (m)

Now try this

To help you learn the food words, write out the Spanish words in two lists: foods that are healthy and foods that are unhealthy. Then memorise ten foods that you like and ten foods that you dislike.

2 Lifestyle

Health (S–Z + verbs)

sal (f)	salt
salado/a	salty, savoury
salchicha (f)	sausage
salchichón (m)	(salami) sausage
salsa (f)	sauce
salud (f)	health
saludable	healthy
sangría (f)	sangría
sano/a	healthy
sardina (f)	sardine
sopa (f)	soup
tabaco (m)	tobacco
tapas (fpl)	tapas
tarta (f)	tart, cake
té (m)	tea
tentación (f)	temptation
tortilla (f)	tortilla, omelette
tostada (f)	piece of toast
uvas (fpl)	grapes
vainilla (f)	vanilla
vegetariano/a	vegetarian
verduras (fpl)	vegetables
vinagre (m)	vinegar
vino (blanco / rosado / tinto) (m)	(white / rosé / red) wine
yogur (m)	yoghurt
zumo (de fruta) (m)	(fruit) juice
acostarse	to go to bed
afectar	to affect
arreglar	to fix
beber	to drink
caerse	to fall (down)
causar	to cause
cenar	to dine
cocinar	to cook
comer	to eat
dejar de (+ inf.)	to stop
desayunar	to have breakfast
despertarse	to wake up
drogarse	to take drugs
dormirse	to go to sleep
emborracharse	to get drunk
encontrarse bien / mal	to feel well / unwell

entrenarse	to train
estar en forma	to be fit
evitar	to avoid
fumar	to smoke
hacer aerobic	to do aerobics
hacer (ejercicio)	to do (exercise)
lavar(se)	to wash (yourself)
levantarse	to get up
limpiar	to clean
mantenerse en forma	to keep fit
mejorar(se)	to improve, get well
morir	to die
oler	to smell
preocuparse	to worry
preparar	to prepare
rehabilitar	to rehabilitate
relajarse	to relax
respirar	to breathe
tener dolor de …	to have a sore …
tener hambre	to be hungry
tener miedo	to be afraid
tener sed	to be thirsty
tener sueño	to be sleepy
tomar	to take

Health

alcoholismo (m)	alcoholism
alimentación (f)	food
apetecer	to fancy, feel like
ataque cardíaco (m)	heart attack
aviso (m)	advice
cerebro (m)	brain
drogadicto/a (m/f)	drug addict
esfuerzo (m)	effort
fumador pasivo (m)	passive smoker
hervido/a	boiled
hígado (m)	liver
merluza (f)	hake
olor (m)	smell
porro (m)	joint
respiratorio/a	respiratory
sabroso/a	tasty

seropositivo/a	HIV positive
síndrome de abstinencia (m)	withdrawal
sustancia química (f)	chemical substance
tabaquismo (m)	smoking
vena (f)	vein
advertir	to advise
dar de comer	to feed
cansar	to get tired
correr el riesgo	to run the risk
hacer daño	to do damage
inyectar(se)	to inject (yourself)
provocar	to cause, provoke

Relationships and choices (A–B)

abuelo/a (m/f)	grandfather/ mother
activo/a	active
adolescente	adolescent
adolescente (m/f)	teenager
adoptivo/a	adopted
adulto/a (m/f)	adult
agresivo/a	aggressive
alegre	happy
amable	kind
ambicioso/a	ambitious
amigo/a (m/f)	friend
amor (m)	love
anciano/a	old
anciano/a (m/f)	old man / woman
animado/a	lively
animal doméstico (m)	pet
antipático/a	unpleasant
apellido (m)	name, last name
aspecto (m)	appearance
atención (f)	attention
barba (f)	beard
bebé (m)	baby
beneficio (m)	benefit
beso (m)	kiss
bigote (m)	moustache
boca (f)	mouth
brazo (m)	arm

Now try this

Pick out ten verbs from this page and write each of them in the past, present and future tenses in the 1st person singular (I form).

② Lifestyle

Relationships and choices (C–P)

caballo (m)	horse
cabeza (f)	head
calvo/a	bald
canario (m)	canary
carácter (m)	character
cariño (m)	love, affection
cariñoso/a	affectionate
carnet de identidad (m)	identity card
casado/a	married
casamiento (m)	wedding, marriage
castaño	chestnut-coloured
chico/a (m/f)	boy/girl
cómico/a	funny
compañero/a (m/f)	companion, partner
comprensivo/a	understanding
conflicto (m)	conflict
contento/a	content
corto/a	short
creativo/a	creative
cualidad (f)	quality, characteristic
cuidadoso/a	careful
dedo (m)	finger
defecto (m)	defect, flaw
demás, los	the others
deportivo/a	sporting
discriminación (f)	discrimination
discusión (f)	discussion
divorciado/a	divorced
divorcio (m)	divorce
documentación (f)	documentation
edad (f)	age
educado/a	well-mannered
egoísta	selfish
encuesta (f)	survey
extranjero (m)	foreigner
extrovertido/a	extrovert
familia (f)	family

familia adoptiva (f)	adoptive family
felicidad (f)	happiness
feliz	happy
formal	polite, formal
fuerte	strong
gafas (fpl)	glasses
generación (f)	generation
generoso/a	generous
gente (f)	people
gracioso/a	funny
guapo/a	good-looking
hablador(a)	talkative
hermanastro/a (m/f)	half-brother / half-sister, stepbrother / stepsister
hermano/a (m/f)	brother / sister
hijo/a (único/a) (m)	(only) child
hogar (m)	home
hombre (m)	man
honesto/a	honest
honrado/a	honest
identidad (f)	identity
igualdad (f)	equality
impaciente	impatient
incluir	to include
independencia (f)	independence
independiente	independent
influencia (f)	influence
injusto/a	unjust
inmigrante (m)	immigrant
inteligente	intelligent
introvertido/a	introverted
invitación (f)	invitation
invitado/a (m/f)	guest
joven	young person
jubilado/a	retired
justo/a	fair
juventud (f)	young people
largo/a	long
liso/a	straight
loco/a	mad
madrastra (f)	stepmother
madre (f)	mother
maleducado/a	rude
maltrato (m)	abuse
mamá (f)	mum
mano (f)	hand
marido (m)	husband

mascota (f)	pet
matrimonio (m)	marriage
miembro (m)	member
moreno/a	dark-haired
muchacho (m)	boy / girl
mujer (f)	wife, woman
nacido/a	born
nacimiento (m)	birth
nacionalidad (f)	nationality
nariz (f)	nose
necesidad (f)	need
nervioso/a	nervous
nieto/a (m/f)	grandchild
niño/a (m)	(little) boy / girl
nombre (m)	name
novio/a (m/f)	boyfriend / girlfriend
ojo (m)	eye
ONG (f)	NGO (non-governmental organisation)
optimista	optimistic
oreja (f)	ear
orgulloso/a	proud
paciente	patient
padrastro (m)	stepfather
padre (m)	father
padres (mpl)	parents
pájaro (m)	bird
papá (m)	dad
parado/a	unemployed
pareja (f)	couple
paro (m)	unemployment
pecas (fpl)	freckles
pelirrojo/a	red-haired
pelo (m)	hair
perezoso/a	lazy
periquito (m)	parakeet, parrot
persona (f)	person
personalidad (f)	personality
pesimista	pessimistic
pie (m)	foot
pierna (f)	leg
pobre	poor
pobreza (f)	poverty
práctico/a	practical
preferencia (f)	preference
prejuicio (m)	prejudice
primo/a (m/f)	cousin
prudente	wise

Now try this

To help you learn the personality adjectives, write out the Spanish adjectives in three lists: positive, negative and neutral. Then memorise five adjectives that could describe you.

Lifestyle

Relationships and choices (R–Z + verbs)

racismo (m)	racism
racista	racist
reacción (f)	reaction
reservado/a	reserved
responsable	responsible
reunión (f)	meeting
rizado/a	curly
rubio/a	blond-haired
señor (m)	man
señora (f)	woman
señorita (f)	young woman
sensación (f)	sensation
sentido del humor (m)	sense of humour
sentimiento (m)	feeling
separado/a	separated
serio/a	serious
sida (m)	Aids
simpático/a	likeable
sincero/a	sincere
soltero/a	single, unmarried
tímido/a	shy
tío/a (m/f)	uncle / aunt
tolerante	tolerant
tortuga (f)	tortoise
travieso/a	mischievous, naughty
triste	sad
valiente	brave
vandalismo (m)	vandalism
vecino/a (m/f)	neighbour
violencia (f)	violence
violento/a	violent
voluntario/a	voluntary
voluntario/a (m/f)	volunteer
voz (f)	voice
adoptar	to adopt
arruinar	to ruin
beneficiar	to benefit
besar	to kiss
casarse	to get married
conocer	to know, be familiar with
contribuir	to contribute

conversar	to chat
cuidar	to look after
dar las gracias	to thank
decidir	to decide
describir	to describe
destruir	to destroy
discutir	to discuss
divorciarse	to get divorced
educar	to train, educate
enamorarse	to fall in love
enfadar(se)	to be angry
estar en paro	to be unemployed
formar parte de	to be part of
hablar	to speak
inmigrar	to immigrate
jubilarse	to retire
llamarse	to be called
llevar (puesto)	to wear
llevarse bien / mal con	to get on well / badly with
maltratar	to ill-treat
meter	to put
nacer	to be born
ofender	to offend
ofenderse	to be offended
parecerse a	to look like
ponerse	to become
romper	to break (up)
separarse	to separate
supervisar	to supervise
tener (el pelo ... los ojos ...)	to have (... hair / eyes)
tener ... años	to be ... years old
tener suerte	to be lucky

Relationships and choices

amistoso/a	friendly
anillo (m)	ring
atento/a	attentive
atrevido/a	daring
avaro/a	mean, greedy
barrera generacional (f)	generation gap
boda (f)	wedding
callado/a	quiet
cara (f)	face

celoso/a	jealous, keen
cobarde	cowardly
confianza (f)	confidence
cortés	polite
débil	weak
dirección (f)	management
encargado/a (m/f)	manager
enérgico/a	energetic
esposo/a (m/f)	husband/wife
estado civil (m)	marital status
expectativa (f)	prospect
gamberro/a (m/f)	hooligan
gemelo/a (m/f)	twin
género (m)	gender
gerente (m/f)	manager
glotón/ona	gluttonous
huérfano/a (m/f)	orphan
madre soltera (f)	single mother
obra benéfica (f)	charity
parientes (mpl)	relatives
pelea (f)	fight
perspectiva (f)	outlook
residencia (de ancianos) (f)	old people's home
seguro/a de sí mismo/a	self-confident
sensible	sensitive
sin techo (los)	homeless (people)
sobrino/a (m/f)	nephew / niece
temperamento (m)	temperament
testigo (m/f)	witness
torpe	clumsy
vago/a	vague
viudo/a	widowed
acoger	to welcome
agradecer	to thank
aguantar	to endure
cometer	to commit
confiar	to trust, rely on
dedicarse	to be involved in
disculpar(se)	to apologise
emigrar	to emigrate
estropear	to damage, ruin
llorar	to cry
ocuparse de	to take care of
pelear(se)	to fight
perdonar	to forgive
relacionarse con	to be related to
sonreírse	to smile

Now try this

Write out all your family members in Spanish and add a suitable adjective for each of them.

③ Leisure

Free time and the media (A–O)

a mitad de precio	half-price
abrigo (m)	coat
actriz (f)	actress
aficionado/a (m/f)	fan
alpinismo (m)	mountaineering
ambiente (m)	atmosphere
anuncio (m)	advertisement
apto/a	suitable
archivo (m)	file
artículo (m)	article
artista (m/f)	artist
atleta (m/f)	athlete
atletismo (m)	athletics
baile (m)	dance
baloncesto (m)	basketball
banda ancha (f)	broadband
bañador (m)	swimsuit
batería (f)	drums
bicicleta / bici (f)	bicycle / bike
billar (m)	billiards
billete (m)	banknote
blusa (f)	blouse
bolso (m)	(hand)bag
botas (fpl)	boots
boxeo (m)	boxing
caja (f)	till
cambio (m)	change
camisa (f)	shirt
camiseta (f)	T-shirt
campeón/ona (m/f)	champion
campeonato (m)	championship
canción (f)	song
cantante (m/f)	singer
carnicería (f)	butcher's (shop)
carrera (f)	race
cartas (fpl)	playing cards
CD (m)	CD
céntimo (m)	cent
chándal (m)	tracksuit
chaqueta (f)	jacket
cheque (m)	cheque
cibercafé (m)	Internet cafe
ciencia ficción (f)	science fiction
clásico/a	classical

cliente (m/f)	customer
colección (f)	collection
collar (m)	necklace
comedia (f)	comedy
comienzo (m)	beginning
compras (fpl)	shopping
concurso (m)	competition, game show
confitería (f)	confectioner's (shop)
conversación (f)	conversation
copa (f)	cup, trophy
correo basura (m)	junk mail
cosa (f)	thing
de acción	action
de aventura	adventure
deporte (m)	sport
deportista (m/f)	sportsman/woman
deportista	sporty
descanso (m)	rest
descuento (m)	discount
dibujos animados (mpl)	cartoons
dinero (m)	money
disco (compacto) (m)	(compact) disk
disco duro (m)	hard drive / disk
diversión (f)	fun
documental (m)	documentary
droguería (f)	drugstore
educativo/a	educational
entrada (f)	ticket
equipo (m)	team
espectáculo (m)	show, spectacle
estadio (m)	stadium
falda (f)	skirt
fiesta (f)	party
footing (m)	jogging
frutería (f)	greengrocer's (shop)
gafas de sol (fpl)	sunglasses
gol (m)	goal
gorra (f)	cap
Gran Hermano	Big Brother
grandes almacenes (mpl)	department stores
grupo (m)	group, band
guantes (mpl)	gloves
guitarra (f)	guitar
hipermercado (m)	hypermarket

historia (f)	story
instrumento (m)	instrument
joyería (f)	jeweller's (shop)
juego (m)	game
Juegos Olímpicos (mpl)	Olympic Games
jugador/a (m/f)	player
juguete (m)	toy
juguetería (f)	toyshop
juntos/as	together
libra (esterlina) (f)	pound (sterling)
librería (f)	bookshop
lista (f)	list
lotería (f)	lottery
medias (fpl)	media
mensaje (de texto) (m)	(text) message
mercado (m)	market
moda (f)	fashion
monedero (m)	purse
monitor (m)	monitor
monopatín (m)	skateboard
móvil (m)	mobile (phone)
muñeca (f)	doll
música (f)	music
natación (f)	swimming
noticias (fpl)	news
novela (f)	novel
ocio (m)	leisure
oferta (f)	offer
(ordenador) portátil (m)	laptop
ordenador (m)	computer

 calcetines (mpl)

 cinturón (m)

 bufanda (f)

 zapatos (mpl)

 sombrero (m)

 corbata (f)

Now try this

Look at the clothes that you and your friends are wearing today. Check that you can translate them all into Spanish.

③ Leisure

Free time and the media (P-S + verbs)

paga (f)	pocket money
página web (f)	web page
panadería (f)	baker's (shop)
pantalla (f)	screen
pantalón (m)	trousers
pantalón corto (m)	shorts
papelería (f)	stationer's (shop)
paraguas (m)	umbrella
partido (m)	game, match
pasatiempo (m)	pastime
pastelería (f)	cake shop
patinaje (m)	skating
película (f)	film
pelota (f)	ball
peluquería (f)	hairdresser's (shop)
pendientes (mpl)	earrings
perfumería (f)	perfume shop
periódico (m)	newspaper
pesca (f)	fishing
pescadería (f)	fishmonger's (shop)
ping-pong (m)	table tennis
pista de hielo (f)	ice rink
policíaco/a	detective (story, film)
posibilidad (f)	possibility
precio (m)	price
premio (m)	prize
programa (m)	program
programador/a (m/f)	programmer
publicidad (f)	advertising
quiosco (m)	stand, kiosk
ratón (m)	mouse
rebajas (fpl)	sales
recibo (m)	receipt
red (f)	Internet
regalo (m)	gift, present
reloj (m)	watch
resto (m)	remainder
revista (f)	magazine
rico/a	wealthy
robo (m)	theft

romántico/a	romantic
ropa (f)	clothes
sala de chat (f)	chat room
sala de fiestas (f)	night club
salida (f)	outing
sandalias (fpl)	sandals
sección (f)	section
selección (f)	selection
serie (f)	series
sesión (f)	session
sitio web (m)	website
socio (m)	member, partner
solo/a	alone
sonido (m)	sound
supermercado (m)	supermarket
taquilla (f)	box office
tarjeta de crédito (f)	credit card
tebeo (m)	comic
teclado (m)	keyboard
técnico/a (m/f)	technician
telenovela (f)	soap (on TV)
tenis (m)	tennis
tiempo libre (m)	free time
tienda de comestibles (f)	grocery (shop)
tienda de ropa (f)	clothes shop
tipo (m)	type
vaqueros (mpl)	jeans
vela (f)	sail
vendedor/a (m/f)	seller
vestido (m)	dress
videoclub (m)	video club
videojuego (m)	video game
voleibol (m)	volleyball
zapatería (f)	shoe shop
zapatillas de deporte (fpl)	trainers
aceptar	to accept
acompañar	to accompany
acordar	to agree
actuar	to act, take action
ahorrar	to save
andar	to walk
bailar	to dance
borrar	to delete
cantar	to sing
chatear	to chat
coleccionar	to collect
comprar	to buy
conectar	to connect

conectarse	to log / sign in
contar	to count, to tell / recount
correr	to run
costar	to cost
deber	to owe
descargar	download
desconectar	to disconnect
devolver	to return
echar (de menos)	to throw away (to miss)
elegir	to choose
encontrarse	to meet
enviar	to send
escoger	to choose
escuchar	to listen (to)
esperar	to wait
estar de moda	to be in fashion
ganar	to win
gastar	to spend
grabar	to record
guardar	to save
hacer (+ sport)	to do (+ sport)
hacer la(s) compra(s)	to do the shopping
invitar	to invite
jugar	to play
leer	to read
mandar	to send
marcar (un gol)	to score (a goal)
montar	to mount
nadar	to swim
navegar (por Internet)	to surf (the Internet)
necesitar	to need
organizar	to organise
pagar	to pay
participar	to participate
pasear	to walk
paseo, dar un	(to go for a) walk
patinar	to skate
perder	to lose, to miss
pescar	to fish
practicar	to practise
probar(se)	to try (on)
recibir	to receive
regalar	to give away
repartir	to deliver
robar	to steal
saber	to know
salir	to leave, go out
seleccionar	to choose

Now try this

Draw stickmen doing the sports listed and label them in Spanish, to help memorise the words and how to spell them.

③ Leisure

Free time and the media (verbs)

servir	to serve
sugerir	to suggest
tener ganas (de)	to feel like
tocar	to play (an instrument)
tocar	to touch
vender	to sell
venir	to come
ver	to see

Toco la guitarra.
I play the guitar.

Bailo.
I dance.

Leo.
I read.

Cocino.
I cook.

Dibujo.
I draw.

Pinto.
I paint.

Free time and the media

actuación (f)	performance
ajedrez (m)	chess
apodo (m)	nickname
balón (m)	ball
camisón (m)	nightdress
cazadora (f)	jacket
ciberespacio (m)	cyberspace
contraseña (f)	password
de lujo	luxury
electrodomésticos (mpl)	electrical appliances

en efectivo	in cash
estrella (f)	star
función (f)	function
internauta (m/f)	internet user
maquillaje (m)	makeup
medalla (f)	medal
medias (fpl)	tights
panty (m)	tights
prensa (f)	press
rebeca (f)	cardigan
reembolso (m)	refund
reparto a domicilio (m)	home delivery
riesgo (m)	risk
satélite (m)	satellite
sudadera (f)	sweatshirt
surtido (m)	range, assortment
tabacalera (f)	tobacco (trader)
torneo (m)	tournament
usuario/a (m/f)	user
venta (f)	sale
acceder	to agree
adjuntar	to attach
cargar	to load, charge
dar una vuelta	to go for a stroll
hacer cola	to queue (up)
lograr	to achieve
reírse	to laugh
ser aficionado/a a	to be fan of

Holidays (A–D)

abanico (m)	fan
aduana (f)	customs
aeropuerto (m)	airport
agencia de viajes (f)	travel agency
aire acondicionado (m)	air-conditioning
al aire libre	outdoors
albergue juvenil (m)	youth hostel
alemán/ana	German
Alemania	Germany
alojamiento (m)	accommodation
ambiente (m)	atmosphere
América del Sur	South America
andén (m)	platform

Año Nuevo (m)	New Year
asiento (m)	seat
autobús (m)	bus
autocar (m)	coach
autopista (f)	motorway
avión (m)	plane
balcón (m)	balcony
barco (m)	boat
billete (m)	ticket
billete de ida (m)	single (ticket)
billete de ida y vuelta (m)	return (ticket)
británico/a	British
cafetería (f)	cafeteria
cama de matrimonio (f)	double bed
cámara (f)	camera
camino (m)	road, way
camping (m)	campsite
Canarias Islas (fpl)	Canary Islands
caravana (f)	caravan
carnet (m)	pass
carretera (f)	road
carta (f)	menu
castañuelas (fpl)	castanets
castellano/a	Castilian
cheque de viaje (m)	traveller's cheque
cinturón de seguridad (m)	safety belt
(primera) clase (f)	(first) class
coche (m)	car
conductor/a (m/f)	driver, motorist
consigna (f)	left-luggage office
corrida (f)	bullfight
costa (f)	coast
costumbre (f)	custom
crema solar (f)	sun cream
cruce (m)	crossroads
cuchara (f)	spoon
cuchillo (m)	knife
cuenta (f)	bill
cultura (f)	culture
delicioso/a	delicious
deporte (m)	sport
deportes acuáticos (mpl)	water sports
deportes de invierno (mpl)	winter sports
destino (m)	destiny
Día de Reyes (m)	Epiphany (6th January)

Now try this

Choose a holiday or trip you have been on and memorise 10–15 words connected with that holiday or trip.

3 Leisure

Holidays (D–S)

directo/a	direct
documento (m)	document
equipaje (m)	luggage
escocés/esa	Scottish
Escocia	Scotland
España	Spain
español(a)	Spanish
especialidad (f)	specialty
esquí (m)	skiing
estación de autobuses (f)	bus station
estación de trenes (f)	train station
Estados Unidos (mpl)	Unites States
Europa	Europe
europeo/a	European
extranjero/a	foreign
extranjero (m)	abroad
ferrocarril (m)	railway
ficha (f)	card
fiesta (f)	festival
flamenco (m)	flamenco
folleto (m)	brochure
foto(grafía) (f)	photo(graph)
francés/esa	French
Francia	France
(no) fumador	(non-)smoking
Gales	Wales
galés/esa	Welsh
gasolina (f)	petrol
Gran Bretaña	Great Britain
Grecia	Greece
guía (m/f)	guide
guía (f)	guidebook
habitación doble (f)	double room
habitación individual (f)	single room
hamburguesería (f)	hamburger restaurant
heladería (f)	ice-cream parlour
incluido/a	included, including
información (f)	information
Inglaterra	England
inglés/esa	English
insolación (f)	sunstroke
Irlanda	Ireland
irlandés/esa	Irish
isla (f)	island
Italia	Italy
italiano/a	Italian
lado (m)	side
latinoamericano/a	Latin American
libre	available
lista (de precios) (f)	(price) list
llegada (f)	arrival
Londres	London
maleta (f)	(suit)case
mapa (m)	map
máquina de fotos (f)	camera
mar (m)	sea
media pensión	half board
Mediterráneo (m)	Mediterranean
menú del día (m)	menu of the day
menú turístico (m)	tourist menu
metro (m)	underground
mejicano/a (mejicano/a)	Mexican
Méjico	Mexico
montaña (f)	mountain
montañoso/a	mountainous
moto(cicleta) (f)	motorbike
nada más	nothing else
Navidad (f)	Christmas
Nochebuena (f)	Christmas Eve
Nochevieja (f)	New Year's Eve
norteamericano/a	(North) American
oficina de turismo (f)	tourist office
país (m)	country
Papá Noel	Father Christmas
papel higiénico (m)	toilet paper
parada (f)	stop
parador (m)	tourist hotel
parking (m)	car park
parque temático (m)	theme park
pasajero/a (m/f)	passenger
pasaporte (m)	passport
paso subterráneo (m)	underpass
pensión (f)	boarding house
pensión completa	full board
permiso de conducir (m)	driving licence
pista (f)	track
plan (m)	project
plano (m)	map
plato (m)	dish, plate
plato combinado (m)	combo dish
playa (f)	beach
plaza de toros (f)	bullring
portugués/esa	Portuguese
postal (f)	postcard
postre (m)	dessert
primer plato (m)	first course
propina (f)	tip
recepción (f)	reception
recuerdo (m)	souvenir
reserva (f)	booking, reservation
restaurante (m)	restaurant
rueda (f)	wheel
saco de dormir (m)	sleeping bag
sala de espera (f)	waiting room
salida (f)	departure, exit
Semana Santa (f)	Holy Week
señal (f)	sign
servicio (m)	service
servicios (mpl)	toilets
sitio (m)	space, room

una tienda · una caravana · los servicios · el parque infantil · las duchas · un saco de dormir · las canchas de tenis · los árboles

Now try this

List all the countries that you can find on this page, then memorise them. Cover the Spanish and try to write them again, with the correct spellings.

Had a look ☐   Nearly there ☐   Nailed it! ☐

③ Leisure

Holidays (S–Z + verbs)

sombrilla (f)	parasol
sudamericano/a	South American
suplemento (m)	excess fare, supplement
taquilla (f)	ticket office
tenedor (m)	fork
tienda (f)	tent
torero (m)	bullfighter
toro (m)	bull
tradición (f)	tradition
tradicional	traditional
Tráigame …	Bring me …
transporte (público) (m)	public transport
tren (m)	train
turismo (m)	tourism
turista (m/f)	tourist
turístico/a	tourist
vacaciones (fpl)	holidays
vaso (m)	glass
vía (f)	road, way
viaje (m)	journey
viajero/a (m/f)	travellers
visita (f)	visit
visitante (m/f)	visitor
vista (f)	view
vuelo (m)	flight
alojarse	to stay, to lodge
aparcar	to park
bañarse	to bathe, to swim

broncearse	to sunbathe
buscar	to look for
cambiar	to change
caminar	to walk
conducir	to drive
continuar	to continue
cruzar	to cross
dejar	to leave
descansar	to rest
doblar	to turn
esquiar	to ski
estar de vacaciones	to be on holiday
funcionar	to function
informar(se)	to inform (yourself)
ir al extranjero	to go abroad
ir de excursión	to go on a trip
ir de vacaciones	to go on holiday
llegar	to arrive
llevar	to carry
parar	to stop
pasar	to spend time
pedir	to ask for
quedarse	to stay
recomendar	to recommend
recordar	to remember
reservar	to reserve
sacar	to take out
sacar fotos	to take photos
seguir	to follow
tardar	to take time
tomar el sol	to sunbathe
torcer	to twist
traer	to bring
viajar	to travel
visitar	to visit
volver	to return

Holidays

argentino/a	Argentinian
alquiler (de coches) (m)	(car) hire
avería (f)	breakdown
averiado/a	damaged
bonobús (m)	travel card
camión (m)	lorry
carnet de conducir (m)	driving licence
casco (m)	helmet
chileno/a	Chilean
colombiano/a	Columbian
cubano/a	Cuban
disponible	available
DNI	National Identity card
extranjero/a (m/f)	foreigner
motor (m)	engine
peruano/a	Peruvian
queja (f)	complaint
recuerdo (m)	memory
regreso (m)	return
retraso (m)	delay
tranvía (m)	tram
detener(se)	to stop
hacer transbordo	to make a connection, to change
quejarse	to complain
regresar	to return

en el campo
in the countryside

en la montaña
in the mountains

en la playa
at the beach

en la cuidad
in town

España		Spain
Inglaterra		England
Escocia		Scotland
Gales		Wales
Gran Bretaña		Great Britain
Irlanda		Ireland
Francia		France
Alemania		Germany

Now try this

Think of your last holiday. Make a list in Spanish of all the verbs on this page which could apply to that holiday. Then close the book and try to write the English equivalents from memory.

④ Home and environment

Home and local area (A–O)

afueras (fpl)	outskirts
alfombra (f)	carpet
alquilado/a	rented
aniversario (m)	anniversary
aparcamiento (m)	car park
apartamento (m)	apartment, flat
árbol (m)	tree
armario (m)	wardrobe, cupboard
ascensor (m)	lift
aseo (m)	toilet
ayuntamiento (m)	town hall
banco (m)	bank
baño (m)	bath
barrio (m)	district
biblioteca (f)	library
bloque (m)	block
bolera (f)	bowling alley
bosque (m)	forest, woods
butaca (f)	(arm)chair
calefacción (f)	heating
calle (f)	street
cama (f)	bed
campo (m)	field, countryside
cancha (de tenis) (f)	(tennis) court
casa (f)	house
casa adosada (f)	semi-detached / terraced house
castillo (m)	castle
centro (m)	centre
centro comercial (m)	shopping centre
césped (m)	lawn
chalet / chalé (m)	cottage
chimenea (f)	fireplace, chimney
cine (m)	cinema
ciudad (f)	city
club de jóvenes (m)	youth club
cocina (f)	kitchen, cooker
cocina (de gas) (f)	(gas) cooker

cocina eléctrica (f)	electric cooker
comedor (m)	dining room
comisaría (f)	police station
cómodo/a	comfortable
concierto (m)	concert
construcción (f)	building, construction
cortina (f)	curtain
cuarto de baño (m)	bathroom
cumpleaños (m)	birthday
dirección (f)	address
discoteca (f)	discotheque
dormitorio (m)	bedroom
ducha (f)	shower
edificio (m)	building
entrada (f)	entrance
equitación (f)	horse-riding
escalera (f)	stairs, staircase
espacio (m)	space, room
espejo (m)	mirror
esquina (f)	corner
estación de servicio (f)	service station
estanco (m)	tobacconist's (shop)
estante (m)	shelf
estantería (f)	bookcase
estéreo (m)	stereo
fábrica (f)	factory
fiesta (de cumpleaños) (f)	birthday party
flor (f)	flower
fregadero (m)	sink
frigorífico (m)	refrigerator
galería de arte (f)	art gallery
garaje (m)	garage
granja (f)	farm, farmhouse
habitación (f)	room
habitante (m)	inhabitant
histórico/a	historical
iglesia (f)	church
industria (f)	industry
industrial	industrial
jardín (m)	garden
ladrón (m)	thief

lago (m)	lake
lámpara (f)	lamp
lavabo (m)	washbasin
lavadora (f)	washing machine
lavaplatos (m)	dishwasher
librería (f)	bookcase
limpio/a	clean
llave (f)	key
luz (f)	light
manta (f)	blanket
máquina (f)	machine
mesa (f)	table
mezquita (f)	mosque
microondas (m)	microwave
monumento (m)	monument
moqueta (f)	carpet
muebles (mpl)	furniture
museo (m)	museum
nevera (f)	fridge

ayuntamiento (m) town hall

catedral (f) cathedral

centro comercial (m) shopping centre

parque infantil (m) playground

cine (m) cinema

Now try this

Find 20 words on this page that you could use to describe your home and your town. Learn them, then write sentences that use ten of the words.

④ Home and environment

Home and local area (P–Z + verbs)

palacio (m)	palace
papelera (f)	bin
pared (f)	wall
parque (m)	park
parque de atracciones (m)	amusement park
parque infantil (m)	playground
pasillo (m)	hallway, corridor
patio (m)	patio, courtyard
pintado/a	painted
piscina (f)	swimming pool
piso (m)	floor, flat
planta (f)	plant, floor
planta baja (f)	ground floor
plaza (f)	square
polideportivo (m)	sports centre
propio/a	own
provincia (f)	province, county
pueblo (m)	town
puente (m)	bridge
puerta (f)	door
puerto (m)	port, harbour
radiador (m)	radiator
región (f)	region, area
residencial	residential
río (m)	river
ruido (m)	noise
ruidoso/a	noisy
sala de estar (f)	living room
salón (m)	lounge
santo (m)	saint's day, name day
semáforo (m)	traffic light
sierra (f)	mountain range
silla (f)	seat
sillón (m)	(arm)chair
sofá (m)	sofa
sótano (m)	basement, cellar
suelo (m)	floor, ground

teatro (m)	theatre
teléfono (móvil) (m)	(mobile) phone
televisor (m)	television set
terraza (f)	terrace, balcony
tienda (f)	shop
ventana (f)	window
vida (f)	life
zona (f)	zone, area
zona peatonal (f)	pedestrian zone
alquilar	to rent, hire
arreglar	to fix
bajar	to go down
celebrar	to celebrate
coger	to get, catch
compartir	to share
construir	to build
cortar	to cut
cumplir ... años	to turn, reach the age of ...
dar a	to look onto
enseñar	to show

entrar	to go in, enter
montar a caballo	to ride
mostrar	to show
mudarse (de casa)	to move (house)
sentarse	to sit down
subir	to go up
vivir	to live

Home and local area

aldea (f)	village
alquiler (m)	rent
ático (m)	attic
bañera (f)	bath(tub)
concurrido/a	crowded
desván (m)	loft, attic
domicilio (m)	home
horno (m)	oven
persianas (fpl)	blinds
vestíbulo (m)	hall
vivienda (f)	housing, dwelling

un aseo
un cuarto de baño
una cocina
un dormitorio / una habitación
un comedor
un jardín
un salón

el estante / la estantería
the shelf / shelves
el armario
the wardrobe / cupboard
el estéreo
the music system
la silla
the chair
la ventana
the window
la alfombra
the rug
la cortina
the curtain
la moqueta
the carpet
la cama
the bed

Now try this

Make a list in Spanish of all the amenities in your local town, using the vocabulary on this spread to help you.

4 Home and environment

Environment

a pie	on foot
accidente (m)	accident
aire (m)	air
atasco (m)	traffic jam
atmósfera (f)	atmosphere
basura (f)	rubbish
bolsa plástica (f)	plastic bag
campaña (f)	campaign
capa de ozono (f)	ozone layer
cartón (m)	cardboard
contaminación (f)	pollution
contenedor (m)	container
daño (m)	damage
desastre (m)	disaster
destrucción (f)	destruction
ecológico/a	organic, ecological
electricidad (f)	electricity
eléctrico/a	electrical
energía (f)	energy
extinción (f)	extinction
fuego (m)	fire
gasolina sin plomo (f)	unleaded petrol
grave	serious
incendio (m)	fire
medio ambiente (m)	environment
medioambiental	environmental
mundial	worldwide
mundo (m)	world
naturaleza (f)	nature
oxígeno (m)	oxygen
peligro (m)	danger
peligroso/a	dangerous
petróleo (m)	oil
pila (f)	battery
planeta (m)	planet
poco sano	unhealthy

preocupado/a	concerned
problema (m)	problem
productos químicos (mpl)	chemicals
químico/a	chemical
recargable	rechargeable
reciclable	recyclable
reciclaje (m)	recycling
residuos orgánicos (mpl)	organic waste
spray (m)	spray
sucio/a	dirty
Tierra (f)	Earth
tóxico/a	toxic
tráfico (m)	traffic
transporte (m)	transport
uso (m)	use
vehículo (m)	vehicle
apagar	to turn off
ayudar	to help
contaminar	to pollute
dañar	to damage
desaparecer	to disappear
ducharse	to have a shower
encender	to turn on
ensuciar	to pollute
malgastar	to waste
matar	to kill
producir	to produce
proteger	to protect
reciclar	to recycle
recoger	to pick up
reducir	to reduce
reutilizar	to reuse
salvar	to save
separar la basura	to sort the rubbish
tirar	to throw (away)
transportar	to carry
usar	to use
utilizar	to use

Environment

agujero (m)	hole
aumento (m)	increase
calentamiento (m)	warming
CFCs (mpl)	CFCs
combustible (fósil) (m)	(fossil) fuel
consumidor/a (m/f)	consumer
consumo (m)	consumption
culpa (f)	blame
desforestación (f)	deforestation
desperdicio (m)	waste
efecto invernadero (m)	greenhouse effect
envase (m)	packaging
gases de escape (mpl)	exhaust fumes
inquietante	disturbing
inundación (f)	flood
lluvia ácida (f)	acid rain
marea negra (f)	oil slick
petrolero (m)	(oil) tanker
pesticida (m)	pesticide
recurso (m)	resource
selva (f)	forest, jungle
sequía (f)	drought
agotar	to exhaust
amenazar	to threaten
aumentar	to increase
consumir	to consume
echar la culpa	to blame
inquietar(se)	to be worried

Es importante apagar las luces.
It is important to turn off lights.

Es importante usar el transporte publico.
It is important to use public transport.

Now try this

Choose ten verbs you could use when talking about the environment. Write sentences that contain the verbs.

⑤ Work and education

School / college and future plans (A–P)

acento (m)	accent
actividad (f)	activity
alemán (m)	German
alumno/a (m/f)	pupil, student
apoyo (m)	support
apuntes (mpl)	notes
arte dramático (m)	dramatic art
asignatura (f)	subject
aula (f)	classroom
ausente	absent
ayuda (f)	help
bachillerato (m)	baccalaureate
biología (f)	biology
bolígrafo / boli (m)	(ballpoint) pen
calculadora (f)	calculator
campo de deportes (m)	sports field
cantina (f)	canteen
castigo (m)	punishment
chicle (m)	chewing-gum
ciencias (fpl)	science
ciencias económicas (fpl)	economics
clase (f)	class
cocina (f)	food technology
colegio (m)	school
comedor (m)	canteen
comercio (m)	business studies
comportamiento (m)	behaviour
conducta (f)	conduct
consejo (m)	advice
cuaderno (m)	notebook, exercise book
curso (m)	course
deberes (mpl)	homework
desobediente	disobedient
detalle (m)	detail
dibujo (m)	art
diccionario (m)	dictionary
director/a (m/f)	head teacher
diseñar	to draw
educación física (f)	PE
escuela (f)	school
español (m)	Spanish
estricto/a	strict
estuche (m)	pencil case
estudiante (m/f)	student
estudios (mpl)	studies
examen (m)	exam
éxito (m)	success
femenino/a	female
física (f)	physics
físico/a	physical
fracaso (m)	failure
francés (m)	French
geografía (f)	geography
gimnasia (f)	gymnastics
gimnasio (m)	gymnasium
goma (f)	eraser
historia (f)	history
idioma (m)	language
informática (f)	IT, computer science
inglés (m)	English
insolente	insolent
instalaciones (fpl)	equipment, facilities
instituto (m)	college
intercambio (m)	exchange
laboratorio (m)	laboratory
lápices de colores (mpl)	coloured pencils
lápiz (m)	pencil
lección (f)	lesson
lengua (f)	language
letra (f)	letter
libertad (f)	freedom
libro (m)	book
literatura (f)	literature
masculino/a	male
matemáticas (fpl)	mathematics
mixto/a	mixed
mochila (f)	school bag, rucksack
nivel (m)	level
nota (f)	mark
obligatorio/a	compulsory
opción (f)	option
oportunidad (f)	opportunity
optar	to choose
optativo/a	optional
página (f)	page
palabra (f)	word
permiso (m)	permission
pizarra (f)	(black)board
prácticas laborales (fpl)	work experience
pregunta (f)	question
presentación (oral) (f)	(spoken) presentation
presente	present
primario/a	primary
privado/a	private
profesor/a (m/f)	teacher
prueba (f)	test
público/a	public

el arte dramático

el francés

la geografía

la música

la tecnología

el inglés

la historia

la educación física

el dibujo

la informática

las ciencias

las matemáticas

Now try this

What GCSEs are you and your friends taking? Check that you can translate them all into Spanish. If you're thinking of doing some subjects at A level, can you translate those too?

5 Work and education

School / college and future plans (Q-Z + verbs)

química (f)	chemistry
recreo (m)	break
regla (f)	rule, ruler
religión (f)	RE
respeto (m)	respect
respuesta (f)	answer
resultado (m)	result
resumen (m)	summary
sacapuntas (m)	pencil sharpener
sala de profesores (f)	staff room
salón de actos (m)	assembly hall
secundario/a	secondary
severo/a	severe
silencio (m)	silence
sobresaliente	outstanding
taller (m)	workshop
tarea (f)	task
tecnología (f)	technology
tema (m)	topic
texto (m)	text
tijeras (fpl)	scissors
trabajador/a	hard-working
trabajo (m)	job
trabajos manuales (mpl)	manual work
trimestre (m)	term
tutor/a (m/f)	tutor
uniforme (m)	uniform
vestuarios (mpl)	changing rooms
víctima (f)	victim
vocabulario (m)	vocabulary
apoyar	to support
aprender	to learn
aprobar	to approve
atacar	to tackle, strike
callar(se)	to keep quiet
castigar	to punish

charlar	to chat
comenzar	to begin
comprender	to understand
contestar	to answer
dibujar	to draw
empezar	to begin
enseñar	to teach
entender	to understand
escribir	to write
estudiar	to study
faltar	to be absent
fracasar	to fail
golpear	to hit
insultar	to insult
intimidar	to bully
levantar la mano	to raise your hand
mirar	to look at
molestar	to annoy
olvidar	to forget
pasar	to spend
pedir permiso	to ask for permission
preguntar	to ask
prometer	to promise
repasar	to review
respetar	to respect
sacar buenas/ malas notas	to get good/ bad marks
suspender	to suspend, fail
terminar	to finish

School / college and future plans

acoso escolar (m)	bullying
carpeta (f)	folder
carrera (f)	profession
despacho (m)	office
enseñanza (f)	education
riguroso/a	rigorous
comportarse	to behave
entregar	to hand in
ponerse a (+ inf.)	to start
traducir	to translate

Current and future jobs (A-C)

a tiempo completo	full time
a tiempo parcial	part time
abogado/a (m/f)	lawyer
amo/a de casa (m/f)	househusband/ wife
ambición (f)	ambition
arroba	@
azafata (f)	flight attendant
barra (f)	slash
bombero (m)	firefighter
buzón (m)	letterbox
cajero (m)	cashier
calificación (f)	qualification
calificado/a	qualified
camarero/a (m/f)	waiter/waitress
candidato/a (m/f)	candidate
carnicero/a (m/f)	butcher
carpintero/a (m/f)	carpenter
carta (f)	letter
cartero/a (m/f)	postman/woman
cita (f)	appointment
clínica (f)	clinic
cocinero/a (m/f)	cook
comerciante (m/f)	dealer
comercio (m)	commerce, shop
compañía (f)	company
competente	competent
condiciones de trabajo (fpl)	working conditions
contable (m/f)	accountant
contrato (m)	contract
correo (m)	mail
correo electrónico (m)	email
correspondencia (f)	correspondence

abogado lawyer

azafata air hostess

Now try this

Pick five verbs on this spread and write each of them out in the first person form of the future tense.

⑤ Work and education

Current and future jobs (D–Z + verbs)

dentista (m/f)	dentist
dependiente (m/f)	shop assistant
derechos (mpl)	rights
ejército (m)	army
electricista (m/f)	electrician
empleado/a (m/f)	employee
empleo (m)	job
empresa (f)	company
enfermero/a (m/f)	nurse
entrevista (f)	interview
entusiasmo (m)	enthusiasm
escritor/a (m/f)	writer
experiencia laboral (f)	work experience
explicación (f)	explanation
granjero/a (m/f)	farmer
guión bajo (m)	underscore
hombre / mujer de negocios (m/f)	businessman/ woman
horario de trabajo (m)	working hours
horas de trabajo flexibles (f)	flexible working hours
ingeniero/a (m/f)	engineer
intención (f)	intention
intérprete (m/f)	interpreter
jardinero/a (m/f)	gardener
jefe/a (m/f)	boss
laboral	working
línea (f)	line
llamada (f)	call
mecánico/a (m/f)	mechanic
médico (m/f)	doctor
mensaje (m)	message
militar (m/f)	soldier
objetivo (m)	objective
obrero/a (m/f)	worker
oficina (f)	office
panadero/a (m)	baker
participación (f)	participation
peluquero/a (m/f)	hairdresser
periodismo (m)	journalism
periodista (m/f)	journalist
pintor/a (m/f)	painter

policía (m/f)	police officer
preocupación (f)	concern
pronto	ready
punto (m)	dot
puntocom	.com
recepcionista (m/f)	receptionist
responsabilidad (f)	responsibility
salario (m)	wages
secretario/a (m/f)	secretary
sello (m)	stamp
sobre (m)	envelope
soldado (m/f)	soldier
solicitud (f)	application
sueldo (m)	pay
tarjeta (f)	card
teletrabajo (m)	teleworking
título (m)	university degree
trabajador/a (m/f)	worker
traductor/a (m/f)	translator
veterinario/a (m/f)	vet
contactar	to contact
encontrar	to find
explicar	to explain
ganar	to earn
hacer prácticas	to gain work experience
llamar por teléfono	to make a phone call
obtener	to obtain
pagar bien/mal	to pay well/ badly
probar	to have a go, to try
rellenar	to fill in
tomar un año libre / sabático	to take a year off
trabajar	to work

Current and future jobs

albañil (m/f)	builder
aprendiz/a (m/f)	apprentice
camionero/a (m/f)	lorry driver
conseguir	to achieve
ejecutivo/a (m/f)	executive
encargado/a de	in charge of
entusiasta	enthusiastic
estrés (m)	stress
estresante	stressful
llegar a ser	to become
propósito (m)	aim
solicitar	to apply
adjuntar	to enclose
encargarse	to be in charge
estar en huelga	to be on strike
estar estresado/a	to be stressed
hacer un aprendizaje	to do an apprenticeship

bombero
fireman

camarero
waiter

enfermero
nurse

médico
doctor

obrero
worker

veterinario
vet

Now try this

To help you learn the jobs vocabulary, make a list of five jobs that you would like to do and five that you would not like to do. Then memorise them.

Answers

Lifestyle

1. Birthdays
1 A 2 C 3 B

2. Pets
1 T + O
2 T
3 T
4 O

3. Physical description
1 C F
2 D E
3 A

6. Extended family
1 P+N
2 N

9. Breakfast
1 They get good grades / marks.
2 It should be (*two of*) healthy, balanced and tasty.
3 You should avoid tea and coffee as they are stimulants and make you stressed.

10. Eating at home
1 B
2 A

11. Eating in a café
1 P
2 P+N
3 N

12. Eating in a restaurant
B C D

13. Healthy eating
1 C
2 B
3 C

15. Health problems
1 Hard drugs
2 Alcoholism
3 Obesity

16. Future relationships
1 C 2 B

17. Social issues
1 F 2 E

18. Social problems
1 Sofía D
2 Jorge A
3 Laura E

Leisure

19. Hobbies
Laura F
Pablo A
José E

20. Sport
1 D 2 F

21. Arranging to go out
1 A 2 A 3 C

23. TV programmes

Preferred type of programme	Reason
(Pablo) Cartoons	Funnier than documentaries
(María) Gameshows	Less repetitive, more exciting than news

24. Cinema
Sonia P + N
Alberto N
Miguel P

25. Music
1 She's a fan of rock music, and she thinks learning an instrument is one of the hardest things to achieve.
2 Sailing

26. New technology
1 Chatting with friends
2 Sending emails and doing homework.
3 She was spending too much money.

27. Internet language
1 Don't do it ilegally,
2 Send messages to your aunt in the US.
3 The screen and keyboard.
4 Tell anyone what it is.

28. Internet pros and cons
A, B, E

29. Shops
1 5
2 3
3 4
4 1
5 2

30. Shopping for food
1 C
2 A

31. At the market
A C

33. Shopping for clothes

Item	Problem	Colour purchased
1 skirt	Too small	Yellow
2 Shoes	Too big	Brown
3 dress	Dirty / marked	White

34. Returning items
1 It's too small
2 Give him a refund as there is not another black suit
3 To bring his receipt and his credit card

36. Pocket money
1 To buy a new mobile
2 Buy lots of magazines or books
3 She's going to work in a hairdresser's.

39. Booking accommodation
A D F

40. Staying in a hotel
1 C
2 B

41. Staying on a campsite
1 Y
2 Y
3 C
4 C + Y

Home and environment

47. My house
1 C
2 B

49. Helping at home
1 J
2 J
3 E

50. My neighbourhood
1 P
2 P + N

51. Places in town
1 She went to the library to study.
2 She studied at the library that is behind the Sports centre as the school library is too busy.
3 To his grandparents house for supper / to eat at nine o'clock.

52. At the tourist office
1 6
2 5
3 1

54. Signs around town
1 F
2 D
3 B

56. Town description

Name	Problem mentioned	Action required	When
Iván	Not enough buses	Increase number of buses	Next year

57. Weather
1 B
2 B
3 A

59. Directions

Place	Directions given
Bakery	Turn left, second street on the right

60. Transport

Car	D
Coach	A + D

61. At the train station
1 C
2 B
3 C

62. News headlines
1 China
2 Theft of 40 000 credit card numbers

64. Environmental issues
1 E
2 B

Work and education

66. School subjects
1 B
2 C

68. School routine
1 7.30am, 4 pm
2 When it rains
3 To chess club

72. Problems at school
1 B
2 F

75. Jobs
1 30
2 Fireman
3 He didn't like working at night
4 Waiter
5 Builder
6 You can earn a lot of money

76. Job adverts
D F

77. CV
1 C
2 B
3 C
4 C

78. Job application
1 Shop assistant with direct sales to clients' experience
2 Every day, including Sunday but not Mondays.
3 In their clothes shops in the city centre.

79. Job interview
1 Waitress in a Mexican restaurant but she was badly paid.
2 She would prefer to work for a British firm.
3 Sometimes the clients can be unpleasant.
4 Ambitious and never shy.

80. Opinions about jobs
1 Jorge
2 Ramón
3 Ramón

82. My work experience
1 P + N
2 N

84. Dialogues and messages
1 B
2 B

Grammar

85. Nouns and articles
1 **1** folletos **2** veces
3 tradiciones **4** cafés
5 actores
2 **1** la **2** el **3** el
4 la **5** la

86. Adjectives
pequeña, bonitas, ingleses, simpática, habladora, históricos, ruidosos, interesantes

87. Possessives and pronouns
mi, sus, mi, que, su, el mío, él, el suyo

88. Comparisons
1 el peor **2** los mejores
3 la más bonita **4** aburridísimo
5 la mejor **6** el más feo
7 más guapo **8** más perezosa

89. Other adjectives
1 Ese chico es tonto.
2 Esta manzana es rica.
3 Quiero comprar esos vaqueros.
4 Aquella casa es grandísima.
5 Esta película es aburrida.
6 No quiero ese jersey – quiero esa rebeca.

90. Pronouns
1 Voy a darlo a mi padre. / Lo voy a dar a mi padre.
2 La quiero.
3 Voy a comprarlo. / Lo voy a comprar.
4 Los vi en Bilbao.
5 Quiero decirle un secreto.

91. The present tense
1 escucho
2 hablan
3 juega
4 quieres
5 comemos
6 encuentran
7 vivís
8 duerme

92. Reflexives & irregulars
1 **1** Me **2** se **3** me
4 nos **5** te **6** se
2 **1** conozco – I know / meet
2 tengo – I have
3 vamos – we go
4 pongo – I put
5 salgo – I go out
6 traigo – I bring

93. *Ser* and *estar*
1 está **2** es **3** es
4 estoy **5** son **6** es
7 están **8** está

94. The gerund
1 estoy / estaba jugando
2 estoy / estaba escribiendo
3 está / estaba hablando
4 está / estaba durmiendo
5 estoy / estaba comiendo
6 estoy / estaba tomando
7 están / estaban navegando
8 estás / estabas cantando

95. The preterite tense
1 I go to Italy. (present)
2 I arrived at six. (preterite)
3 I surf the internet. (present)
4 He / She listened to music. (preterite)
5 He / She went to a party which was great. (preterite)
6 It was cold and it rained a bit. (preterite)
7 We saw Pablo in the market. (preterite)
8 I played basketball on the beach. (preterite)

96. The imperfect tense
1 trabajaba **2** comí **3** iba
4 había **5** visité **6** lloraba

97. The future tense
1 **1** Nunca fumaré.
2 Ayudaré a los demas.
3 Cambiaremos el mundo.
4 Trabajaré en un aeropuerto.
2 **1** Voy a salir a las seis.
2 Voy a ser médico.
3 Va a ir a España.
4 Mañana voy a jugar al tenis.

98. The conditional
bebería, haría, practicaría, tomaría, bebería, comería, me acostaría, dormiría, llevaría

99. Perfect and pluperfect
1 He visitado Palma con mi novio. (perfect)
2 Han hecho sus deberes con mi ayuda. (perfect)
3 Habíamos ido al supermercado con Pablo. (pluperfect)
4 Mi hermana ha escrito una carta de amor. (perfect)
5 ¿Has visto mi abrigo? perfect
6 Cuando llegó, mis primos habían comido ya. (pluperfect)

100. Giving instructions
1 Write to me.
2 Wait for your sister.
3 Don't tell me.
4 Don't shout!
5 Click here.
6 Don't take photos!
7 Answer the questions.
8 Don't leave everything to the last minute.

101. The present subjunctive
1 When I go to university, I'll study French.
2 I don't think your friend is good looking.
3 When I'm 18, I'll take a gap year.
4 I want you to talk to Pablo.
5 It's not true that English food is horrible.
6 I don't think Italy is the best football team.

102. Negatives
Suggested answers:
1 No como nunca verduras.
2 No tengo ningún libro.
3 No conozco a nadie.
4 Nadie juega a pelota.
5 Nunca hago mis deberes.
6 No me gusta ni navegar por Internet ni descargar música.
7 No tiene nada.
8 No tengo ningún amigo en Londres.

103. Special verbs
1 Me duele
2 Le gusta
3 Me gustaron
4 Les hace falta
5 Le duelen
6 Me encanta
7 Nos quedan
8 A María le gustan

104. *Por* and *para*
1 1 para   **2** para   **3** por
  4 para   **5** para   **6** por
  7 por
2 1 para   **2** por   **3** para
  4 por   **5** ✓   **6** para
  7 ✓   **8** ✓

105. Questions and exclamations
1 d   **2** f   **3** h   **4** e   **5** a
6 b   **7** c   **8** g

106. Connectives and adverbs
1 *Suggested answers*:
  1 Nunca voy a Paris porque es
    aburrido.
  2 Mientras jugaba al
    baloncesto, Juan hacía
    patinaje.
  3 Después de estudiar, iré a la
    universidad.
  4 Nos gustaría ir a la playa pero
    está lloviendo.
2 1 tranquilamente (peacefully)
  2 perfectamente (perfectly)
  3 difícilmente (with difficulty)
  4 severamente (strictly)

107. Numbers
1 las nueve menos veinte
2 cuatrocientos sesenta y cinco
3 el doce de junio de dos mil
  catorce
4 séptimo
5 las once y media
6 setenta y seis
7 el primero / el uno de enero de
  mil novecientos noventa y siete
8 tercero

Your own notes

Your own notes

Published by Pearson Education Limited, Edinburgh Gate, Harlow, Essex, CM20 2JE.

www.pearsonschoolsandfecolleges.co.uk

Text © Pearson Education Limited 2013
Audio recorded at Tom Dick + Debbie Productions, © Pearson Education Limited
MFL Series Editor: Julie Green
Edited by Siân Mavor and Sue Chapple
Typeset by Kamae Design, Oxford
Original illustrations © Pearson Education Limited 2013
Illustrated by John Hallet, KJA Artists
Cover illustration by Miriam Sturdee

The rights of Leanda Reeves and Tracy Traynor to be identified as authors of this work have been
asserted by them in accordance with the Copyright, Designs and Patents Act 1988.

The authors and publishers are grateful to Ian Kendrick for permission to use original material.

First published 2013

16 15 14 13
10 9 8 7 6 5 4 3 2

British Library Cataloguing in Publication Data
A catalogue record for this book is available from the British Library

ISBN 978 1 447 94118 7

Printed and bound by L.E.G.O. S.p.A. Lavis (TN) - Italy

Acknowledgements
The author and publisher would like to thank the following individuals and organisations for
permission to reproduce photographs:

(Key: b-bottom; c-centre; l-left; r-right; t-top)
Alamy Images: Andalucia Plus Image bank 11, Cultura Creative 64c, David Grossman 17, ©
FORGET Patrick / SAGAPHOTO.COM 29l, Johner Images 64r, Ken Welsh 29c, Neil Juggins
65b, Photos12 24, Picture Partners 7, 71, Pixoi Ltd 80l; Corbis: Design Pics 93; **Getty Images:**
Marilyn Angel Wynn 79; **Pearson Education Ltd:** Studio 8 86, 90, 75, Jon Barlow 78, Sophie
Bluy 5, 22 / 2, 52, 67, 69, 80r, 89, Gareth Boden 21, MindStudio 29r, 83r, 87, 87 / 2, 87 / 3, 88,
Tudor Photography 16, Jules Selmes 12, 22, 104; **Shutterstock.com:** Darren Blake 96, debr22pics
104 / 2, Fedor Selivanov 64t, Joe Gough 9, Joshua Haviv 95, Monkey Business Images 84,
Natalia Barsukova 39, photobank.ch 65t, PhotoBarmaley 42, Przemyslaw Ceynowa 34, RamonaS
93t, Roberaten 53, Stephen Mcsweeny 34l, Willee Cole 77, Yuri Arcurs 74; **Studio 8:** 45;
Veer / Corbis: AndiPu 50bl, Artur Kotowski 11cl, gem photography 81, hoch2wo 73, Joerg Beuge
10, Kuzma 50, Leaf 82l, lightpoet 82r, Morgan Lane Photography 63, Phase4Photography 50br,
Prochasson Frederic 55, Warrengoldswain 83l

All other images © Pearson Education Limited

Every effort has been made to contact copyright holders of material reproduced in this book. Any
omissions will be rectified in subsequent printings if notice is given to the publishers.

In the writing of this book, no AQA examiners authored sections relevant to examination papers
for which they have responsibility.